The 500 Hidden Secrets of

VANCOUVER

INTRODUCTION

This book was created to help you find the Vancouver that not everyone experiences. It invites you to step off the beaten track and discover places that aren't featured in regular city guides. While it does mention where you'll find the best city view or where to go for fine dining, within its pages you'll also find the best spot for late-night poutine, where to go kayaking by moonlight and where to drink cocktails from a conch shell. This book was made with those places in mind.

Vancouver has a lot to offer, for example a diverse culinary scene and a mosaic of cultures. It's also an ideal destination for those looking to get outside; that's why this guide stretches beyond the downtown city limits and includes many of the best and lesser-known ways to experience the local flora and fauna. Thankfully the city's unique geography makes doing so easy. The Vancouver skyline is an unbelievable mix of modern architecture juxtaposed against a spectacular mountain and ocean background.

This guide does not include everything you can see and do in Vancouver; such an exhaustive list just does not exist. However, this book does highlight a curated selection of the tried-and-true places that Vancouverites have come to treasure. Everything the author has recommended in this book are things she would tell to a dear friend. She hopes you will come to love this city as much as she does.

HOW TO
USE THIS BOOK?

———

This book lists 500 things you need to know about Vancouver in 100 different categories. Most of these are places to visit, with practical information to help you find your way. Others are bits of information that help you get to know the city and its habitants. The aim of this guide is to inspire, not to cover the city from A to Z.

The places listed in the guide are given an address, including the neighbourhood, and a number. The neighbourhood and number allow you to find the locations on the maps at the beginning of the book: first look for the map of the corresponding neighbourhood (for example West End or Gastown), then look for the right number. A word of caution however: these maps are not detailed enough to allow you to find specific locations in the city. You can obtain an excellent map from any tourist office or in most hotels, and of course you can locate the addresses on your smartphone.

Please bear in mind that cities change all the time. The chef who hits a high note one day may be uninspiring on the day you happen to visit. The hotel ecstatically reviewed in this book might suddenly go downhill under a new manager. Or the bar recommended as one of 'the locals' 5 favourite spots for a drink' might be empty on the night you visit. This is obviously a highly personal selection. You might not always agree with it. If you want to leave a comment, recommend a spot or reveal your favourite secret place, please follow @500hiddensecrets on Instagram or Facebook and leave a comment. And of course it's always a good idea to visit our website *www.the500hiddensecrets.com*, where you'll find lots of new content, freshly updated info and travel inspiration.

THE AUTHOR

Shannon McLachlan was born and raised in Vancouver. Having worked in marketing and as a content creator for nearly 10 years, her work has brought her to all corners of the city. She considers herself a mountain-loving, coffee-drinking, photo-taking explorer, constantly curious and on the lookout for new discoveries.

An avid traveller, spending months and years abroad has helped her appreciate all that makes Vancouver unique. Since then she has come to see the city in a new way – with the insight of a local and the perspective of a tourist. She realizes that trying to document and experience everything this dynamic city has to offer is futile, but loves trying anyways.

Naturally, being a true Vancouverite, Shannon enjoys spending time on the hiking trail as much as she does walking the local neighbourhoods. If you ask her, a perfect day in Vancouver starts with a good coffee and a morning hike. It involves a beautiful view and finishes with an evening of delicious food and drinks, preferably paired with another beautiful view.

The author is incredibly grateful to her friends, family, colleagues and acquaintances for sharing their favourite, often secret, spots around the city. Many of them joined her as she scoured streets and photographed location after location. Shannon would also like to thank the business owners of Vancouver she met, as well as Luster's fantastic publishing team, but especially Dettie Luyten. Without her guidance and hard work, this guide would not be what it is.

VANCOUVER

overview

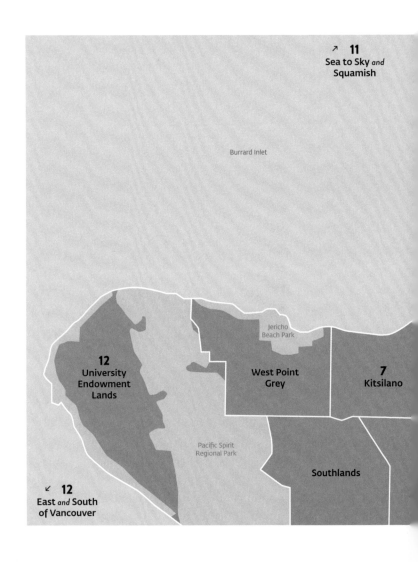

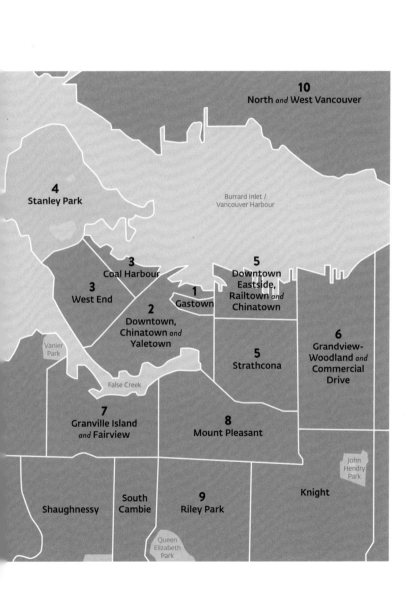

10
North *and* West Vancouver

4
Stanley Park

Burrard Inlet /
Vancouver Harbour

3
Coal Harbour

3
West End

2
Downtown,
Chinatown *and*
Yaletown

1
Gastown

5
Downtown
Eastside,
Railtown *and*
Chinatown

Vanier
Park

False Creek

5
Strathcona

6
Grandview-
Woodland *and*
Commercial
Drive

7
Granville Island
and Fairview

8
Mount Pleasant

John
Hendry
Park

Shaughnessy

South
Cambie

9
Riley Park

Knight

Queen
Elizabeth
Park

Map 1
GASTOWN

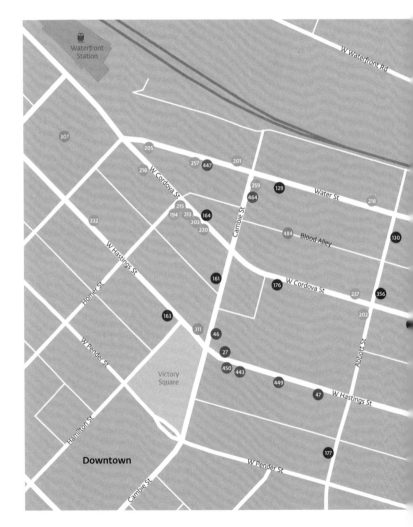

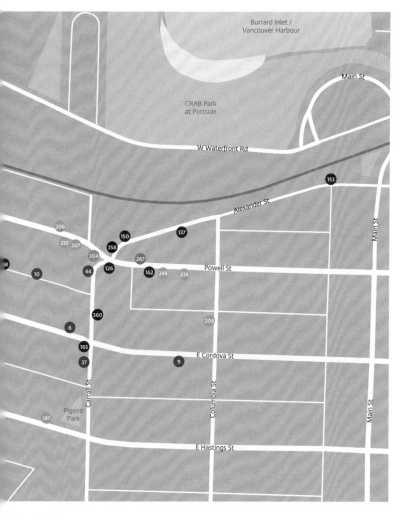

Burrard Inlet /
Vancouver Harbour

Main St

CRAB Park
at Portside

W Waterfront Rd

Alexander St

153

206

210 207

150

137

358

304

126

267

8

44

Powell St

10

162 244 236

360

209

6

165

E Cordova St

37

9

Carrall St

Columbia St

Main St

Pigeon
Park

197

E Hastings St

Map 2
DOWNTOWN *and*
YALETOWN

CHINATOWN

Map 3
WEST END

COAL HARBOUR

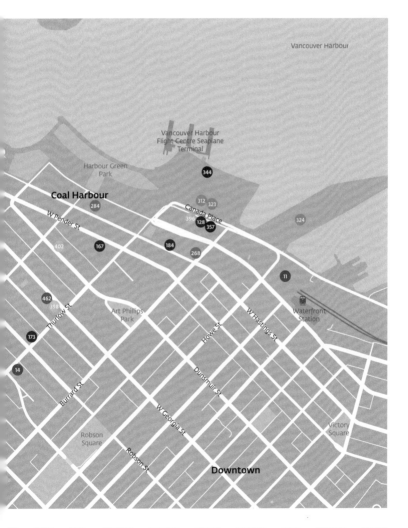

Vancouver Harbour

Vancouver Harbour
Flight Centre Seaplane
Terminal

Harbour Green
Park

Coal Harbour

W Pender St

Canada Place

Art Phillips
Park

Waterfront
Station

Thurlow St

Burrard St

Howe St

W Hastings St

Dunsmuir St

W Georgia St

Robson
Square

Victory
Square

Robson St

Downtown

344
312 323
284
396 128 357
324
402 167 184
268
11
462 398
173
14

Map 4
STANLEY PARK

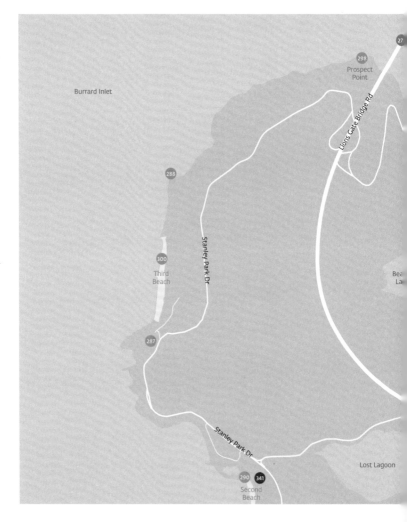

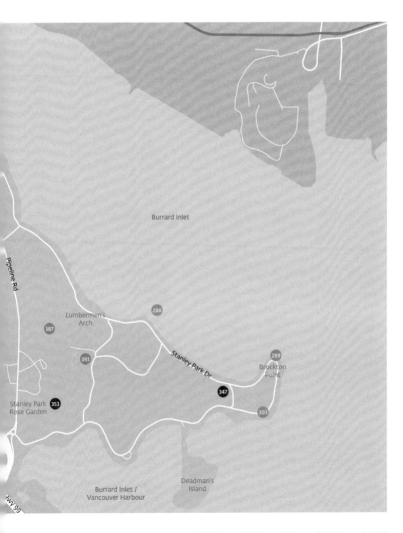

Burrard Inlet

Pipeline Rd

Lumbermen's
Arch

387

393

286

Stanley Park Dr

289
Brockton
Point

347

303

Stanley Park 353
Rose Garden

Deadman's
Island

Burrard Inlet /
Vancouver Harbour

HWY 99

Map 5
DOWNTOWN EASTSIDE, RAILTOWN, CHINATOWN *and* STRATHCONA

EAT — **DRINK** – SHOP – BUILDINGS – DISCOVER – **CULTURE** – CHILDREN – SLEEP – WEEKEND – RANDOM

Map 6
GRANDVIEW-WOODLAND
and COMMERCIAL DRIVE

EAT — DRINK — SHOP — BUILDINGS — DISCOVER — CULTURE — CHILDREN — SLEEP — WEEKEND — RANDOM

Map 7
KITSILANO

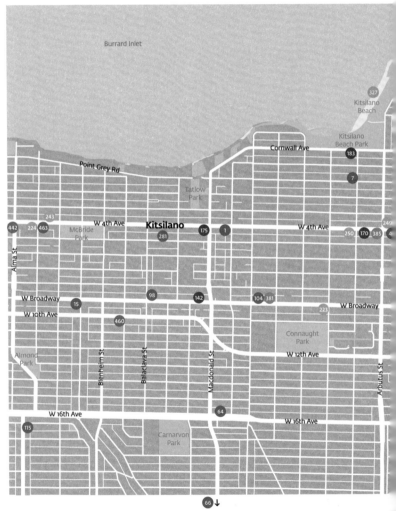

Burrard Inlet

327
Kitsilano Beach

Kitsilano Beach Park
183

Cornwall Ave

Point Grey Rd

7

Tatlow Park

243
442 224 463
W 4th Ave
Kitsilano
281
175
1
W 4th Ave
250 170 385
249
4

Alma St
McBride Park

W Broadway
15
98
142
104 381
223
W Broadway
W 10th Ave
460

Blenheim St
Balaclava St
Macdonald St

Connaught Park

W 12th Ave

Almond Park

Arbutus St

W 16th Ave
115
64
W 16th Ave

Carnarvon Park

66 ↓

GRANVILLE ISLAND, SOUTH
GRANVILLE *and* FAIRVIEW

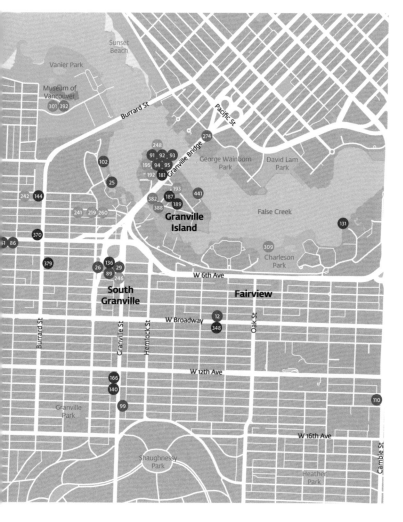

Map 8
MOUNT PLEASANT

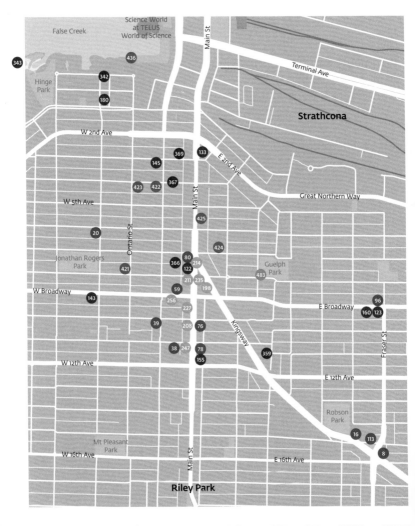

EAT — **DRINK** — SHOP — BUILDINGS — DISCOVER — **CULTURE** — CHILDREN — SLEEP — WEEKEND — RANDOM

Map 9
RILEY PARK

Map 10
NORTH VANCOUVER
and WEST VANCOUVER

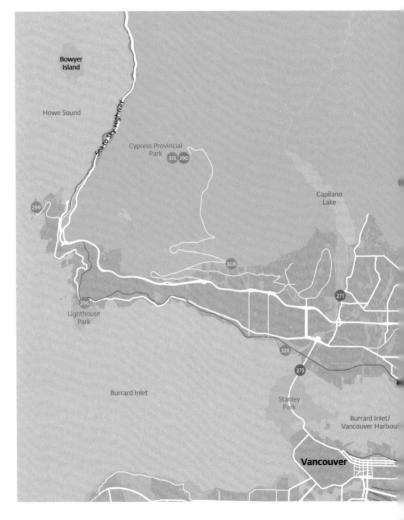

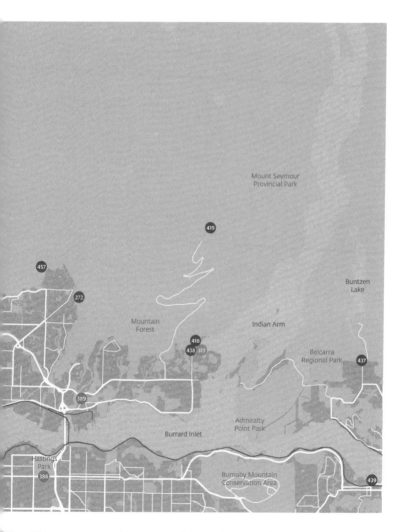

Mount Seymour
Provincial Park

419

457

272

Buntzen
Lake

Mountain
Forest

Indian Arm

416
438 313

Belcarra
Regional Park

437

389

Admiralty
Point Park

Burrard Inlet

Hastings
Park

386

Burnaby Mountain
Conservation Area

439

Map 11
SEA TO SKY
and SQUAMISH

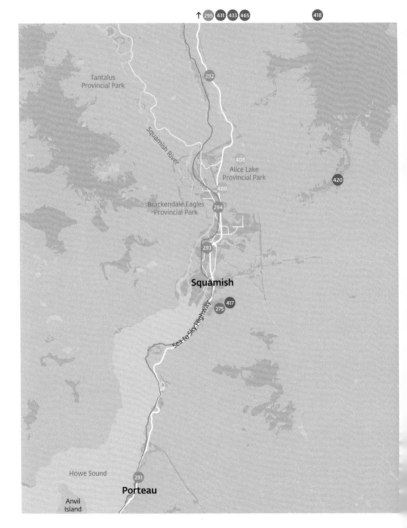

↑ 295 431 433 465   418

Tantalus
Provincial Park

Squamish River

292

406

Alice Lake
Provincial Park

420

400

294

Brackendale Eagles
Provincial Park

293

Squamish

275 417

Sea to Sky Highway

Howe Sound

291

Porteau

Anvil
Island

Map 12

EAST and SOUTH
OF VANCOUVER

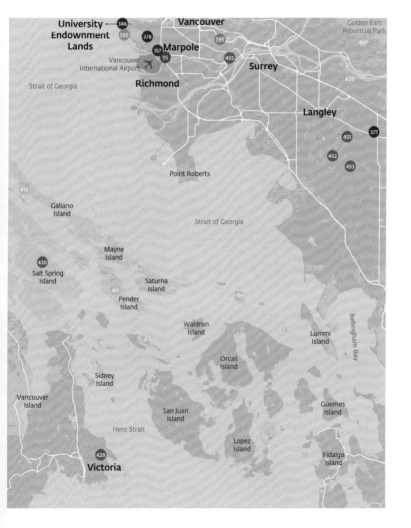

L'ABATTOIR

115 PLACES TO EAT OR BUY GOOD FOOD

The 5 best
VEGETARIAN
restaurants

─────────

1 **THE NAAM RESTAURANT**

2724 W 4th Avenue
Kitsilano ⑦
+1 604 738 7151
thenaam.com

Opened in 1968, The NAAM is the city's oldest natural foods restaurant and a Vancouver institution. Known for their miso gravy and fries, the space is homey and welcoming. The best part? The cafe is open 24 hours a day, 7 days a week, perfect for all your late-night veggie cravings.

2 **THE ACORN**

3995 Main St
Riley Park ⑨
+1 604 566 9001
theacornrestaurant.ca

Named one of the best vegan-friendly restaurants in the world, The Acorn offers veggie-forward fine dining and carefully crafted cocktails. With a seasonal menu, each dish is built around a single, locally sourced ingredient, and promises that even the biggest carnivores won't miss the meat.

*Pro-tip: Check out their sister restaurant, The Arbour, a couple of doors down.

3 KOKOMO

3 KOKOMO

611 Gore Avenue
Chinatown ⑤
+1 604 428 6599
heykokomo.ca

Inspired by the sun, Kokomo is on a mission to bring energy and warmth to everyday life through their refreshing and colourful menu. The plant-based cafe serves up Insta-worthy bowls and smoothies, which taste just as good as they look. Start your day off right with an açai bowl topped with their house-made granola.

4 MEET ON MAIN

4288 Main St
Riley Park ⑨
+1 604 696 1010
meetonmain.com

The gang at MeeT are on a mission to prove that comfort food can be not only delicious and affordable but also vegetarian! The restaurant hosts a large menu and is known for its big burgers, droolworthy poutine and original bowls. Don't miss out on the Sweet-Chili Cauliflower to start.

5 BEETBOX

1074 Davie St
West End ③
+1 604 233 8269
beetboxveg.com

Did someone say vegan comfort food? Beetbox on Davie serves 100% plant-based vegan eats with menu items including burgers, wraps, sandwiches and tasty sides like chili cheeze fries and roasted broccoli with mushroom XO sauce. Intrigued? One look at their droolworthy Instagram (@beetboxveg) will have you heading their way.

The 5 hottest spots for
TACOS

6 **TACOFINO**
15 W Cordova St
Gastown ①
+1 604 899 7907
tacofino.com

What started as a food truck on Vancouver Island is now a Vancouver institution. Inspired by bold flavours, Tacofino has taken the best of surf grub and infused it with West Coast vibes. Their tacos are a no-brainer, but don't miss out on the nachos, margaritas and Diablo Cookies also.

6 TACOFINO

7   LUCKY TACO

1685 Yew St
Kitsilano ⑦
+1 604 739 4677
luckytaco.ca

Located steps away from the beach, Lucky Taco is a semi-authentic taqueria with a seriously good happy hour. Their commitment to using well-raised meat, sustainable seafood and local seasonal ingredients makes for fresh and delicious tacos. Pair your taco with a flight from their impressive tequila and mezcal selection.

8   SAL Y LIMÓN

701 Kingsway St, #5
Mount Pleasant ⑧
+1 604 677 4247
salylimon.ca

Craving authentic Mexican? Sal y Limón is your answer. This casual restaurant is known for being cheap, tasty and having a line out the door. You can't go wrong with a taco but take a peek at the *huraches:* thick homemade corn tortillas, topped with beans, cabbage, red onion, jalapeños, chunky salsa, sour cream, and cheese.

9   LA MEZCALERIA

68 E Cordova St
Gastown ①
+1 778 379 6447
lamezcaleria.ca

Named after the mezcal spirits made from the agave plant, this hip and trendy restaurant pairs great food with a great atmosphere. Try a mezcal flight or opt for a finely crafted cocktail. Whatever you do, don't miss the Queso Fundido — their take on a molten cheese fondue.

10   GRINGO

27 Blood Alley Sq
Gastown ①
+1 604 673 0513
gringogastown.com

Gringo is an upbeat, inexpensive taco bar that loves a little neon. Tucked away down Blood Alley, you can guarantee this spot will play the best of the 1980s and 1990s music, has cheap beer and great tacos. Grab a trucker hat, cozy up to a lawn flamingo and chow down.

5 great places for
JAPANESE FOOD

11 **MIKU**
200 Granville St, #70
Coal Harbour ③
+1 604 568 3900
mikurestaurant.com

Miku serves up sustainable sushi with stunning water views. Famous for being an *aburi* sushi pioneer, *aburi* literally translated means 'flame-seared'.
This technique paired with the freshest seafood and signature sauces make Miku one of the favourite sushi spots in Vancouver.

12 **TOJO'S**
1133 W Broadway
Fairview ⑦
+1 604 872 8050
tojos.com

You may not have heard of chef Hidekazu Tojo but you have likely heard of his food. Born and trained in Japan, chef Tojo moved to Vancouver in 1971 and introduced Omakase cuisine to the city. Credited for creating the California Roll, the Great BC Roll and the Rainbow Roll amongst many others, chef Tojo has earned the title of Master Chef.

13 RAMEN DANBO

1333 Robson St
West End ③
+1 604 559 8112
ramendanbo.com

Ramen Danbo serves up traditional Fukuoka-style Kyushu Hakata Tonkotsu ramen, a perfect warm-up for a grey Vancouver day. Their signature Tonkotsu broth is made in-house daily with simple umami and specially treated, impurity-free water. On the menu you'll also find the insanely spicy Rekka Ramen and vegan versions of everything.

14 GUU

838 Thurlow St
West End ③
+1 604 685 8817
guu-izakaya.com

Guu was the first *izakaya* (Japanese tapas) restaurant to open up in the city. With a focus on authenticity, the restaurant aims to refuel its patrons with good food and atmosphere. They offer tasty dishes at affordable prices, with most items under 10 dollar. Guu is a great spot to share food and drink beer with friends.

15 GREEN LEAF SUSHI

3416 W Broadway
Kitsilano ⑦
+1 604 568 9406

While this small sushi cafe may seem unassuming, the menu is not. Like most sushi restaurants they offer a wide variety of sashimi and sushi rolls; however, Green Leaf is one of the few spots you can find aburi sushi, made popular at the high-end Japanese restaurants, at a reasonable price. The signature salmon *oshi* is a flamed-seared bite of heaven.

5 delicious
ITALIAN
restaurants

---

16 SAVIO VOLPE
615 Kingsway
Mount Pleasant ⑧
+1 604 428 0072
saviovolpe.com

Since opening in 2015, Savio Volpe has made a name for itself as one of the best eateries on the West Coast. Styled after the osterie of Italy, the restaurant serves simple, flavourful food, sourcing ingredients locally while remaining true to their countryside traditions.

17 CAFFE LA TANA
635 Commercial Dr
Commercial Drive ⑧
+1 604 428 5462
caffelatana.ca

Stepping into this 'old world alimentari' feels like stepping back in time. Located on the northern end of Commercial Drive, the cafe offers a small but stunning menu and a selection of fine Italian imports and goods, including in-house freshly made pasta and pastries.

18 PIZZERIA FARINA
915 Main St
Strathcona ⑤
+1 604 681 9334
pizzeriafarina.com

Stepping inside this cozy, bustling pizzeria feels a little bit like you've left Vancouver and wound up in Brooklyn. The Neapolitan-inspired menu is concise but thoughtful, offering a new special each week. Grab a seat in the small dining space surrounded by whitewashed brick and high top tables or take some 'za to go.

19 ASK FOR LUIGI

305 Alexander St
Railtown ⑤
+1 604 428 2544
askforluigi.com

Known for its family-style service and fresh handmade pasta, Ask for Luigi is casual and intimate. All of the dishes are meant to be shared and placed in the centre of the table as they are ready. The space is cozy, tucked inside a small wooden house with a checkered floor and boasts an impressive gluten-free pasta option. Indulge in a slice of olive oil cake to finish.

20 MANGIA CUCINA & BAR

2211 Manitoba St
Mount Pleasant ⑧
+1 604 620 5445
mangiacucina.com

Opened in 2018, Mangia is chef-owned and -operated by Sicilian-born Alessandro Riccobono. Located in a red converted heritage house, the restaurant is casual but cozy and offers an array of contemporary Italian dishes. Chef Alessandro's vision is to bring the tastes of his childhood to Vancouver, and he does it very well.

17 CAFFE LA TANA

The 5 best
SEAFOOD *spots*

21 **HOOK SEABAR**

1210 Denman St
West End ③
+1 604 620 4668
hookseabar.com

Hook delivers on two things: great seafood and great scenery. This smart but laidback restaurant has a stunning West End water view but not stunning prices. The menu is approachable and tasty with classic items like fish and chips, tacos to surf and turf. A great spot for happy hour, the patio always has a busy buzz!

22 **BLUE WATER CAFE**

1095 Hamilton St
Yaletown ②
+1 604 688 8078
bluewatercafe.net

It's impossible to talk about seafood in Vancouver without mentioning this restaurant. Considered the king of seafood, Executive Chef Frank Pabst and his team are consistently voted 'Best Seafood Restaurant' in town. This fine dining experience includes a raw bar, on-ice selections and unprecedented service.

23 FANNY BAY OYSTER BAR AND SHELLFISH MARKET

762 Cambie St
Downtown ②
+1 778 379 9510
fannybayoysters.com

When it comes to eating raw oysters, freshness is not just nice, it's critical. Owned by Fanny Bay Oysters, a B.C. shellfish farming and exporting company, this is the only tide-to-table oyster bar in the city. Undoubtedly the freshest oysters around, get here for happy hour from 3 pm to 6 pm.

24 THE FISH COUNTER

3825 Main St
Riley Park ⑨
+1 604 876 3474
thefishcounter.ca

Co-owned by chef Robert Clark and marine biologist Mike McDermid, this seafood spot serves only local and sustainable seafood. A former Vancouver Aquarium employee, McDermid helped to spearhead the Ocean Wise program. The upbeat restaurant is half retail space, half eatery. The menu varies depending on what's available but bouillabaisse and dairy-free clam chowder are standouts.

25 GO FISH

1505 W 1st Avenue
Granville Island ⑦
+1 604 730 5040

While located incredibly close to Granville Island, this charming seaside shack is technically a 5-minute stroll along Island Park Walk towards Fisherman's Wharf. The vibrant blue hut caters to local fishermen and has a small patio and selection of outdoor seating. More importantly, they have good seafood grub (read: fish and chips) and a great view.

5 not-to-miss places for
SWEET EATS

---

26 BEAUCOUP BAKERY & CAFÉ

2150 Fir St
South Granville ⑦
+1 604 732 4222
beaucoupbakery.com

After working her way up from intern to lead pastry chef and receiving a scholarship to the prestigious École Gastronomique Bellouet Conseil in Paris, Betty Hung took over ownership of Beaucoup Bakery and Café in 2017 with her brother Jacky. The bakery creates exceptional French-inspired pastries, the croissants are hailed as the best in the city and the cafe is bright and beautiful.

27 PUREBREAD

159 W Hastings St
Gastown ①
+1 604 563 8060
purebread.ca

The first thing you'll notice when you step into purebread is the overwhelming smell of butter and sugar. The second thing you'll notice is the never-ending display of droolworthy baked goods. Originally established in Whistler, this family-owned bakery offers an incredible selection of freshly baked goodies. The hardest part is deciding what to have.

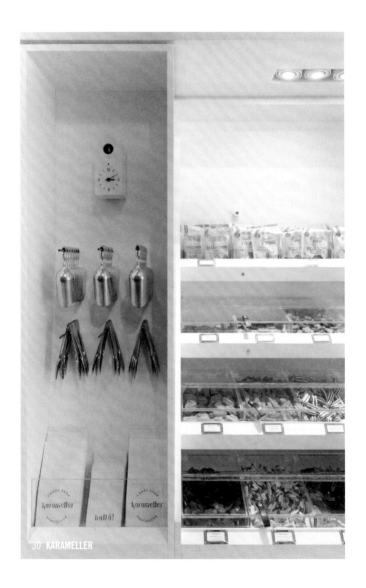

30 KARAMELLER

28 CARTEMS DONUTS

534 W Pender St
Downtown ②
+1 778 708 0996
cartems.com

Handmade from scratch by skilled pastry chefs, Cartems Donuts boasts some of the best donuts in the city. They focus on quality ingredients, creative flavours and making people smile one donut at a time. Try one of their limited specialty flavours or stick with a staple, like the Vanilla Bean, Apple Fritter or the beautiful Earl Grey donut.

29 CHEESECAKE ETC.

2141 Granville St
South Granville ⑦
+1 604 734 7704
cheesecakeetc.com

Mike and Edith Sims travelled the world for 20 years playing jazz music before settling in Vancouver in 1979. They then decided to pull inspiration from their favourite joints and open their own spot for jazz... and cheesecake, their secret family recipe cheesecake to be exact. Open for dessert every day, the space is dimly lit and romantic.

30 KARAMELLER

1020 Mainland St, #30
Yaletown ②
+1 604 639 8325
karameller.com

After making the move to Vancouver from Sweden, Karameller owner-operator Louise opened the Scandinavian sweet shop as an ode to her childhood. Karameller, translated from Swedish, means 'hard candy'. The trendy Yaletown shop imports all of its products from Scandinavia and all are made from high-quality ingredients, and are free of GMOs, trans fats and high-fructose corn syrup.

5 places for a lovely
BRUNCH

---

31 CAFÉ MEDINA

780 Richards St
Downtown ②
+1 604 879 3114
medinacafe.com

This Middle Eastern-inspired bistro has an old-world feel. Staple menu items here include Israeli couscous, paella and fricassee-sunny eggs, braised short ribs, roasted potatoes and smoked cheddar. The most famous menu item however is the Liège-style waffles. Pair them with milk chocolate lavender and white chocolate pistachio rosewater.

32 BANDIDAS TAQUERIA

2781 Commercial Dr
Commercial Drive ⑥
+1 604 568 8224
bandidastaqueria.com

This vegetarian joint serves fresh, Mexi-inspired food. Brunch menu items include delicious breakfast burritos and tacos, but in our opinion, it's all about the eggs Benny, it's served on top of house-made cornbread muffins with pinto beans, roasted yam, potato hash and salsa.

33 THE RED WAGON RESTAURANT

2296 E Hastings St
Grandview-
Woodland ⑥
+1 604 568 4565
redwagoncafe.com

This is a casual but cozy diner serving up nostalgic comfort food. Don't let the long line stop you, the team is pretty good at moving people through, besides the food is worth the wait. Favourites include: pulled pork pancakes, thick Reuben sandwiches, and smoked salmon scrambles.

34 **HUNNYBEE BRUNCHEONETTE**

789 Gore Avenue
Strathcona ⑤
hunnybeebrunch.com

Hunnybee is homey but hip, serves good coffee and tasty bites. Their egg and avocado on sourdough toast with pickled cabbage and *furikake* is delightful, especially when paired with an Orange Blossom Mimosa. This spot is cheerful without being annoying, just how mornings should be.

35 **SLICKITY JIM'S**

3475 Main St
Riley Park ⑨
+1 604 873 6760
skinnyfatjack.com

With walls covered in peculiar art and antiques, Slickity Jim's is that quirky breakfast joint that everybody loves. The star of Slickity's menu is the 10 different eggs Benedict options. Popular picks include A Figment of My Imagination with fig chutney and brie and the Motor Benny with chorizo, bacon, ham and cheddar.

34 HUNNYBEE BRUNCHEONETTE

5 CAFES
you'll find hard to leave

---

36 **LIVIA SWEETS**

1399 Commercial Dr
Commercial Drive ⑥
+1 604 423 3869
liviasweets.com

Step inside this darling cafe and you'll be overcome with the scent of fresh sourdough and coffee. Offering baked goodies, brunch, lunch and some dinner services, Livia began in local farmers' markets around the city. Claire, the brainchild behind it all, can be seen in her signature stripes bustling around the cafe.

37 **NELSON THE SEAGULL**

315 Carrall St
Gastown ①
+1 604 681 5776
nelsontheseagull.com

Warmly lit with natural and string lighting, comfortable furniture and an open kitchen, this cafe is nothing but cozy. Adding to the charming and homey decor is their delicious coffee, baked goods, and food. Their bread is the absolute star of the menu and should be tried at all costs.

38 **DOCK LUNCH**

152 E 11th Avenue
Mount Pleasant ⑧
+1 604 879 3625

Owner Elizabeth Bryan used to live in this quaint and quirky spot prior to its rezoning, which allowed for food service. Serving homemade comfort food, every day the handwritten wall menu is updated with the day's specials. Visiting Dock Lunch is like stopping by a friend's for a wholesome bite and catch up.

39 THE FEDERAL STORE

2601 Quebec St
Mount Pleasant ⑧
+1 778 379 2605
federalstore.ca

Tucked away one block back from
bustling Main Street you'll find this small,
quiet and calm cafe. Originally a family-
run bakery, it became a corner store in
1962 and eventually the hybrid of both
it is now in 2016. Serving quality coffee,
baked goods and food, the cafe sticks
to its roots and also sells a small selection
of groceries.

40 LE MARCHÉ ST. GEORGE

4393 St George St
Riley Park ⑨
+1 604 565 5107
lemarchestgeorge.com

A cafe, a general store, a gathering place
and a home, Le Marché St. George occupies
a small corner on a neighbourhood street
in Riley Park. This rustic-chic cafe is small
but incredibly charming, with an almost
otherworldly feel to it. They serve up
all the goods a quality cafe should have
but their standout is the quiche. Do not
miss out it!

36 LIVIA SWEETS

The 5 best restaurants for
FINE DINING

41 **HAWKSWORTH RESTAURANT**

801 W Georgia St
Downtown ②
+1 604 673 7000
hawksworth restaurant.com

Based in the elegant Rosewood Hotel Georgia, Hawksworth is another Vancouver institution. Opened in 2011, the restaurant serves ingredient led Pacific Northwest cuisine, highlighting the city's cultural environment and the natural surroundings. Executive Chef David Hawksworth is known for his perfectionism and delivers night after night.

42 **ST. LAWRENCE**

269 Powell St
Railtown ⑤
+1 604 620 3800
stlawrence restaurant.com

Comfortable fine dining is a thing and you'll find it at St. Lawrence. Serving classic French cuisine with Quebecois influence, the menu is inspired by chef J-C Poirier's childhood growing up in Quebec and the Montreal restaurant scene. Described as "haute country cooking at its finest", the setting is intimate but dynamic.

43 KISSA TANTO

263 E Pender St
Chinatown ⑤
+1 778 379 8078
kissatanto.com

Going for dinner at Kissa Tanto is like entering a parallel universe. Located on the top floor of a dated Chinatown building, the restaurant pairs the comfort of Italian food with the precision of Japanese. Many would think this pair odd, but Executive Chef Mr. Wanatabe, who is both Italian and Japanese, is an expert. Everything here has a quirky elegance.

44 L'ABATTOIR

217 Carrall St
Gastown ①
+1 604 568 1701
labattoir.ca

Built in the 19th century, this restaurant is situated between the historic Blood Alley and Gaoler's Mews, the site of Vancouver's first jail and former meatpacking district. Serving French-inspired Pacific Northwest cuisine, the menu changes weekly depending on what's available. The space is equal parts elegant and rugged, with the tables in the glass atrium being our particular favourite.

45 ANCORA WATERFRONT DINING AND PATIO – FALSE CREEK

1600 Howe St, #2
Downtown ②
+1 604 681 1164
ancoradining.com

Pairing the best of Japanese and Peruvian cuisine with a stunning view, Ancora is a dining experience only found in Vancouver. Executive Chef Ricardo Valverde and chef Yoshihiro Tabo work together to create a balanced hybrid menu, which includes a selection of ceviches and sushi. The bi-level restaurant features crystal chandeliers and coastal inspired tones.

5 restaurants for
MEAT EATERS

---

46 MEAT & BREAD

370 Cambie St
Gastown ①
+1 604 566 9003
meatandbread.com

This is not your average sandwich shop. Meat & Bread offers hearty, artisanal creations with their signature porchetta sandwich, served with crackling and mustard to dip, at the forefront. The rest of the small but thoughtful menu has a variety of specials that keep things interesting. Grab you sandy from the bar and take a seat at the giant communal table.

46 MEAT & BREAD

47 WILDEBEEST

120 W Hastings St
Gastown ①
+1 604 687 6880
wildebeest.ca

Embracing the field-to-farm movement, Wildebeest utilizes classic butchery with contemporary techniques. First thing on the menu you'll notice is *omakase*, a Japanese expression for 'trust the chef'. The menu states this is the best way to experience Wildebeest and we agree, just be sure to try a bone marrow luge shot, too.

48 ELISA

1109 Hamilton St
Yaletown ②
+1 604 362 5443
elisasteak.com

With over 21 different cuts of steak available, Elisa's is known for its unique and feminine take on the traditional steakhouse experience. Each perfectly cut steak is prepared by Executive Chef Andrew Richardson over a wood-fired grill. In addition to steak, the menu features five variations of tartare.

49 HUNDY

2042 W 4th Avenue
Kitsilano ⑦
+1 604 736 8828
hundy.ca

This burger joint is sneaky. With just four booths hidden behind a sliding wall inside of the cafe Their There, Hundy is only open Thursday through Sunday evenings when the cafe section is closed. They offer a small but mighty menu of burgers and chicken sandwiches.

50 JUKE FRIED CHICKEN

182 Keefer St
Chinatown ⑤
+1 604 336 5853
jukefriedchicken.com

Don't let the hip and lofty space fool you, Juke turns out some mean fried chicken. The buttermilk marinade and gluten-free batter mixed and matched with their original sauces keep things interesting. If you can't dine in, grab a Juke sandwich to go – topped with a droolworthy dill slaw.

The 5 best places for
POUTINE

---

51 FRITZ EUROPEAN FRY HOUSE
718 Davie St
Downtown ②
+1 604 684 0811
*fritzeuropean
fryhouse.com*

See the line-up out the door of Fritz as a good omen. Small and open very late, their award-winning fries are hand cut from Canadian grown potatoes. The poutinerie is also known for its large list of dips to indulge in, including Cajun ketchup, parmesan peppercorn and jalapeño mustard.

52 LA BELLE PATATE
1215 Davie St
West End ③
+1 604 569 1215
iwantpoutine.com

Serving up authentic Quebecois poutine, La Belle Patate also has a lengthy and impressive menu of topping options and flavours. If you're new to the ooey-gooey dish (or really really hungry) this is the only place in the city that has all-you-can-eat poutine on the menu.

53 HARBOUR OYSTER + BAR
1408 Commercial Dr
Commercial Drive ⑥
+1 604 251 6900
harbouryvr.com

We like Harbour for its fresh and delicious seafood but we love it for its lobster poutine. Chow down on some fries covered in jalapeños, corn, cheesy bechamel, more cheese and of course lobster. The vibe here is fun and relaxed, serving all day brunch and a good happy hour.

54 **TAKO**
601 Expo Boulevard
Chinatown ②
+1 778 379 7010
takovancouver.com

A Korean taco joint for poutine? Yep, you read that. This Korean-Mexican fusion restaurant located next to the Stadium-Chinatown SkyTrain station offers a whole menu of tasty mixes, but their take on traditional Canadian cuisine is what we're here for. Their *kimchi* and *bulgogi* poutine is what we want and we want it now.

55 **CAFE DE L'ORANGERIE**
1320 W 73rd Avenue
Marpole ⑫
+1 604 266 0066
cafedelorangerie.ca

For a new and original take on poutine make the trip to this Marpole restaurant. This Italian-Japanese fusion joint replaces the traditional gravy with one of two options: Japanese curry or Japanese stew. Both are exceptional but once you try the curry it's hard to pick anything else. The restaurant is small and affordable.

52 **LA BELLE PATATE**

5 authentic
CHINESE
restaurants

---

56 **BAO BEI**

163 Keefer St
Chinatown ⑤
+1 604 688 0876
bao-bei.ca

Located in Chinatown, this restaurant describes itself as a Chinese 'brasserie' offering a modern approach to an ancient cuisine. Dishing out small sharing plates, chef and owner Tannis Ling has taken inspiration from Taiwan, Shanghai and Sichuan. Favourites: steamed buns with Hunan beef belly and sesame flatbread.

57 **SUN BO KONG**

1363 Kingsway
Knight ⑥
+1 604 255 8927
sunbokong.com

Eating veggies is better for you and the planet, and Sun Bo Kong is on a mission to get you to eat more of them! Serving an array of noodle dishes, fried rice, dim sum, dumplings, soup, congee, and more, this vegetarian Chinese restaurant is an easy sell, even to meat eaters.

58 **SUN SUI WAH**

3888 Main St
Riley Park ⑨
+1 604 872 8822
sunsuiwah.ca

About as authentic as it gets, Sun Sui Wah is known all around the Lower Mainland as the place to go for dim sum and Cantonese cuisine. The large dining room is filled with round tables and regularly full. The menu is extensive, with steamed pork and shrimp *shui ma*, and pan-fried potstickers, being popular table pleasers.

59 CONGEE NOODLE HOUSE

141 E Broadway
Mount Pleasant ⑧
+1 604 879 8221
congeenoodlehouse.com

Opened past midnight every day, this restaurant describes itself as a "no-frills eatery". They serve a wide selection of Chinese cuisine; however, the shining star here is, no surprise, their congee and noodles. The service here is ok, and the menu is affordable, reliable and extensive, boasting over thirty different types of congee.

60 CHINATOWN BBQ

130 E Pender St
Chinatown ⑤
+1 604 428 2626
chinatownbbq.com

With lacquered roasted ducks and soy-steamed chickens hanging in the windows, just walking by this spot is enough to get your mouth watering. Serving traditional and affordable Hong Kong-style barbecue, the beef brisket here is award-winning. The space has a 1960s vibe with checkered floors, emerald green wood and red leather upholstery.

60 CHINATOWN BBQ

5 places for delicious
ICE CREAM

---

61 RAIN OR SHINE
1926 W 4th Avenue,
#102
Kitsilano ⑦
+1 604 428 7246
rainorshineicecream.com

Inspired by the fresh, pure ingredient ice cream they had while travelling, co-owners of this beloved ice-cream parlour Josie Fenton and Blair Casey purchased a make-at-home ice-cream machine and got to work. Opening Rain or Shine in 2013, they work with a local dairy farm to produce the best of the best and have a variety of seasonal flavours.

62 LA CASA GELATO
1033 Venables St
Strathcona ⑤
+1 604 251 3211
lacasagelato.com

A Vancouver legend, La Casa Gelato has been scooping ice cream for Vancouverites for nearly 40 years. Having concocted over 518 flavours with 238 available at any given time, picking just one or two is no small feat. Sampling is welcomed, heck – it's expected. Some of the abnormal flavours include garlic, wasabi, balsamic vinegar and sour cream.

63 UMALUMA

235 E Pender St
Chinatown ⑤
+1 604 559 5862
umaluma.com

A healthy, organic, non-dairy alternative to gelato exists? Yes, and Umaluma is where you'll find it. Developing each recipe from scratch using house-made nut mylks, the 'ice cream' here is as smooth, creamy and flavourful as the real deal stuff. The 100% plant-based parlour has 35 flavours and counting.

64 LA GLACE

2785 W 16th Avenue
Kitsilano ⑦
+1 604 428 0793
laglace.ca

One of the best and most beautiful ice-cream parlours in Vancouver, La Glace produces a French-style ice cream. Made from scratch, they start with a creme anglaise base, a thick custard composed of egg yolks and heavy cream. The finished product is rich and luxurious. The bright interior with gold, white and Tiffany blue accents is a dream.

65 EARNEST ICE CREAM

1485 Frances St
Grandview-
Woodland ⑥
+1 604 428 2933
earnesticecream.com

An institution in the city, Earnest scoops up small-batch ice cream. Staple flavours include London Fog, Whiskey Hazelnut and Matcha Green Tea, in addition to an impressive list of seasonal flavours and rotating specials. There are a couple locations, but this one is our favourite as it's further off the beaten track and generally less busy.

The 5 tastiest
CHEAP EATS

66 **THE PATTY SHOP**
   4019 Macdonald St
   Arbutus Ridge ⑦
   +1 604 738 2144

Husband-and-wife duo Marilyn and Daryl McHardy have been serving up Jamaican patties for more than four decades. The filled half-moon pastries are served over the counter and it is to-go only. The traditional curry beef is always reliable, but the vegetarian curried potatoes, peas and corn is an equally good pick.

67 **FALAFEL KING**
   1110 Denman St
   West End ③
   +1 604 669 7278

This small, to-go spot has been satisfying diets of all types for over 30 years. Located in the West End, Falafel King serves some of the best falafel in town, obviously, but also some delicious meat options including chicken and lamb. There is major bang for your buck here, portion sizes are big!

68 DD MAU

1239 Pacific Blvd
Yaletown ②
+1 604 684 4446
ddmau.ca

Literally translating to 'go go fast', DD Mau specializes in modern Vietnamese *bánh mì* sandwiches and vermicelli noodle bowls. This spot is small, lunch and counter service only, but the food is flavourful, refreshing and affordable. If you're looking for more of a sit-down experience, check out their newer and bigger location in Chinatown.

69 THE DOWNLOW CHICKEN SHACK

905 Commercial Dr
Commercial Drive ⑥
+1 604 283 1385
dlchickenshack.ca

Fried, fresh chicken is king here, and aside from a small offering of tasty side dishes, that's all you'll find. The counter-service spot offers fried chicken either on its own or in a bun, with a variety of creative sauces and escalating spice levels. If you really want to go for it, hit them up for 2 dollar Wing Wednesday.

70 EL FURNITURE WAREHOUSE

989 Granville St
Downtown ②
+1 604 677 8080
warehousegroup.ca

All food items on the menu at the Warehouse are 5,95 dollar. Yes, you read that right, 5,95 dollar. The food at this Granville Street bar is not only cheap but also good, with decent portions and variety. You don't even have to think about splurging on dessert, you just might as well.

5
FOOD TRUCKS
to look for around town

---

71 ROLLING CASHEW
rollingcashew.ca

Vancouver's favourite vegan food truck got its start in 2015 with chef Thibault and his vegetarian crew. You will not miss the meat with this 100% plant-based menu. Our favourites? The Thai cashew chicken, potato croquettes served with either spicy, garlic or tartar cashew sauce and Wednesday Wings Night.

72 JAPADOG
japadog.com

You can't talk about food carts without talking about Japadog. Established in 2005 by a newly immigrated Japanese couple, Japadog has found major success and now operates a number of stands and trucks, with the original still on the corner of Burrard and Smithe. All dogs are good, but the Terimayo is their signature for a reason.

73 THE PRAGUERY
praguery.com

After moving to Vancouver, owner Jaro introduced *trdelník*, a traditional Czech street food, to the city. Made from rolled dough wrapped around a stick, then grilled and topped with sugar, the *trdelník* can be enjoyed on its own, with a spread filling, or with soft served ice cream.

74 **CHICKPEA**
ilovechickpea.ca

Chickpea is the classic tale of a very successful food truck turned very successful restaurant and food truck. The 100% vegan, plant-based menu has a Middle Eastern influence, with hummus being the main staple. Chickpea fries are a must here. The food truck is definitely the original but find their bricks-and-mortar location on Main Street.

75 **VIA TEVERE – IL SALTIMBOCCA**
viateverepizzeria.com

While the restaurant Via Tevere serves some of the city's best Neapolitan pizza, their food truck specializes in Saltimbocca, a 'pizzeria sandwich'. After the bread has been baked in the 900-degree wood-fired oven, it's then loaded with meat and cheese, roasted over the fire and topped with fresh arugula and tomato.

72 JAPADOG

5 fab restaurants that have **SOMETHING FOR EVERYONE**

---

76 **THE CASCADE ROOM**
   2616 Main St
   Mount Pleasant ⑧
   +1 604 709 8650
   thecascade.ca

Describing themselves as a "modern take on a classic UK pub", this Main Street spot has menu items ranging from schnitzel to rigatoni. In addition to their good and wholesome food, they also offer an impressive list of beer, wine and cocktails. Get here for happy hour!

77 **THE RED ACCORDION**
   1616 Alberni St
   West End ③
   +1 604 428 6464
   theredaccordion.com

This restaurant is tucked inside a rust-red West End home. The interior matches the literal homey exterior, with mixed-matched furniture and warm and rich textures. It almost feels like you're having a meal at your favourite aunt's house. Naturally, they serve comfort food favourites. Check out the coffee bar downstairs.

78 LUCY'S EASTSIDE DINER

2708 Main St
Mount Pleasant ⑧
+1 604 568 1550
lucyseastsidediner.com

Open 24 hours, this is East Van's take on the classic neighbourhood diner. Using the freshest ingredients available, they whip up traditional diner dishes with an unexpected flair. The interior is quintessential retro diner. Go here for all-day breakfast, homemade soups, burgers, milkshakes and the like.

79 THE BELGARD KITCHEN

55 Dunlevy Avenue
Railtown ⑤
+1 604 699 1989
belgardkitchen.com

Sharing the Settlement Building with Postmark Brewing, Belgard serves creative local fare. The food here is thoughtful and innovative, with the Yam Gnocchi with Lamb Ragu being one of our personal favourites. The space is lofty, warmed up with the large wood barrels, Edison lights and a fireplace.

80 THE RUMPUS ROOM

2301 Main St
Mount Pleasant ⑧
+1 604 708 0881
rumpusroom.ca

There truly is something here for everyone but where The Rumpus Room really shines is with original twists on old favourites and tasty fried bites. Give the PB&J burger and deep-fried pickles a go! The interior is a groovy throwback with wood panelling, amber pendant lighting, and brown, orange and yellow wallpaper. Like the menu, they somehow make it work.

5 *succesful*
MULTICULTURAL
MASH-UPS

---

81 UGLY DUMPLING
1590 Commercial Dr
Commercial Drive ⑥
+1 604 258 0005
uglydumpling.ca

Serving Pan-Asian fare, co-owners chef
Darren Gee and sommelier Van Doren
Chan hail from some of the finest
restaurants in the city. What makes the
Ugly Dumpling so special? The creative
menu changes daily, you can take part in
the staff's 'family meal' and the dumplings
are often made by Chan's grandma.

82 THE UNION
219 Union St
Chinatown ⑤
+1 604 568 3230
theunionvancouver.ca

The Union dishes out a bold, modern
take on Southeast Asian favourites.
Located in Chinatown, the flavourful food
is served on long, communal tables and
paired with a strong drink list. The *bánh
mì* is a no-brainer and the *kimchi* fries with
gochujang mayo is a must.

83 PHNOM PEHN

244 E Georgia St
Chinatown ⑤
+1 604 734 8898
phnompehn
restaurant.ca

A local legend, this spot arguably serves the best Cambodian and Vietnamese food in the city. The family-owned joint is best known for their highly addictive chicken wings and pepper sauce, but all choices are good choices here. The deep dining room is decorated with Southeast Asian artwork and trinkets.

84 CUCHILLO

261 Powell St
Railtown ⑤
+1 604 559 7585
cuchillo.ca

From the outside, Cuchillo looks very unassuming, with a purple neon skull being the only giveaway to what could be inside. Serving Latin American small plates, this edgy, industrial-chic spot is a great place to share food with friends. The menu features ceviches, tacos, tapas, *antojitos* (Mexican street food) and dulce de leche with churros for dessert.

85 HAVANA

1212 Commercial Dr
Commercial Drive ⑥
+1 604 253 9119
havanavancouver.com

Inspired by the colours and vibes of Old Havana in Cuba, this spot serves Cuban food with Carribean and Pacific Northwest influences. The tropical interior is full on but tasteful. Why not do dinner and a show? Tucked behind the restaurant is an intimate 60-person-seat theatre.

5 *excellent*
FARM-TO-TABLE
restaurants

---

86 FABLE
1944 W 4th Avenue
Kitsilano ⑦
+1 604 732 1322
fablekitchen.ca

Farm + Table = Fable. Inspired by the surrounding community, the kitchen produces inventive, 'creative meets modern' cuisine. The menu changes seasonally depending on what's available. The space is warm and understated but, for an even more casual experience, check out Fable Diner on Broadway.

87 FORAGE
1300 Robson St
West End ③
+1 604 661 1400
foragevancouver.com

Located in the boutique Listel Hotel, Forage connects diners with local farmers, fishers and foragers. Under head chef Welbert Choi, they serve tapas-style plates divided on the menu by their respective beginnings: Soil, Land and Sea. Snacks and Sweets are also on the menu and so is a selection of local beer and wine.

88 THE MACKENZIE ROOM
415 Powell St
Railtown ⑤
+1 604 253 0705
themackenzieroom.com

This contemporary farm-to-table restaurant, led by chef Sean Reeve, serves Pacific Northwest cuisine. On the wall you'll find the chalkboard menu with dishes that change through the season. The food is served family-style and the space is a mix of rustic and refined.

89 FARMER'S APPRENTICE

1535 W 6th Avenue
South Granville ⑦
+1 604 620 2070
farmersapprentice.ca

A minimalist eatery, owner and chef David Gunawan is a true original. Everything on the menu, which changes daily depending on the farmers, comes from organic and ethical farms. There is meat on the menu but it is definitely veggie heavy. The space is small, but whimsical with only 30 seats.

90 ROYAL DINETTE

905 Dunsmuir St
Downtown ②
+1 604 974 8077
royaldinette.ca

Pairing a comfortable atmosphere with good, locally sourced food, Royal Dinette makes farm-to-table approachable. The menu, prepared by chef Amanda Healey is ever-changing, showcasing the best of seasonal ingredients. With checkered floors and a wrap-around bar, the interior is an homage to the bygone diner era.

88 THE MACKENZIE ROOM

93 LEE'S DONUTS

The 5 best **STALLS IN THE GRANVILLE ISLAND MARKET**

91 **THE STOCK MARKET**
1689 Johnston St
Granville Island ⑦
+1 604 687 2433
thestockmarket.ca

When it comes to soups, stocks and sauces, these people are the specialists. Handmade in their market kitchen every day, the shop serves up hot soups to enjoy immediately and also has a wide selection of products to take home. The menu changes daily with fish, meat and veggie options always available.

92 **BENTON BROTHERS FINE CHEESE**
1689 Johnston St
Granville Island ⑦
+1 604 609 0001
bentonscheese.com

Former engineers, Benton brothers Jonah and Andrew opened their doors in 2007. Since then this family-owned and -operated cheese shop has worked with talented cheesemakers, bringing the best of the best to the Granville Island shoppers. Each cheese is hand-selected and staff members are always on hand to chat origins, pairings and flavours.

93 LEE'S DONUTS

1689 Johnston St
Granville Island ⑦
+1 604 685 4021
leesdonuts.ca

A mom-and-pop donut shop, Lee's has been serving handmade donuts based on owners Alan and Betty-Ann Lee's recipe since 1979. The donuts are made fresh throughout the day and often served warm. All their donuts are delicious but the jelly donut, with its balance of textures and flavours, has been dubbed a 'perfect food' by celebrity chef David Chang.

94 GRANVILLE ISLAND TEA COMPANY

1689 Johnston St
Granville Island ⑦
+1 604 683 7491
granvilletea.com

Selling over 200 types of tea, the Granville Island Tea Company was established in 1999 by owners Deborah and Mark Mercier. Their signature black tea tins containing leaves from all over the world line the walls of the shop, reaching up to the ceiling. It's not really a visit unless you have their secret recipe Masala Chai Latte to go.

95 SIEGEL'S BAGELS

1689 Johnston St
Granville Island ⑦
+1 604 685 5670
siegelsbagels.com

When Montreal native Joel Siegel moved to Vancouver and found no good bagel shops, he got in business. Baking constantly throughout the day and night, the bagels here are filling, chewy, boiled and baked to perfection every time. They have a variety of bagel and cream cheese flavours as well as a menu of bagel sandwiches.

5
GOURMET GROCERS
worth a visit

---

96 **NADA**
    675 E Broadway
    Mount Pleasant ⑧
    +1 778 806 3783
    nadagrocery.com

Nada specializes not in a certain food per se, but in a way of life. Literally translating to 'Nothing', Nada is a completely package free grocery store. Customers to the bright and welcoming store will find endless tubs of bulk food, household cleaners, fruits and veggies and a deli. To buy something, just bring your reusable containers and get weighing.

97 **BOSA FOODS**
    562 Victoria Drive
    Grandview-
    Woodland ⑥
    +1 604 216 2659
    bosafoods.com

After recognizing there was a lack of traditional Italian food in the Lower Mainland, Augusto Bosa founded Bosa Foods in 1957. Since then, Bosa's has been importing traditional and specialty Italian food products, originally serving the growing Italian community but now to all Vancouverites. Needing more space, they opened another location on Kootenay Street in East Van in 2006.

98 PARTHENON MARKET
3089 W Broadway
Kitsilano ⑦
+1 604 733 4191

Offering Mediterranean and European specialty foods, Parthenon imports their own exclusive oils, vinegars, olives and the like directly from Greece and other European countries. Come shopping hungry, one side of the shop is isles of food and a deli, the other side is a cafe with a wide selection of authentic Greek food. The hummus is always a yes.

99 MEINHARDT FINE FOODS
3002 Granville St
South Granville ⑦
+1 604 732 4405
meinhardtfinefoods.com

Established in 1996, Meinhardt is a food and flower emporium showcasing the tastiest gourmet foods from around the world. In addition to their products that 'feed your curiosity' they also have delicious ready-to-eat meals and phenomenal desserts, all with a true neighbourhood market feel.

100 THE GOURMET WAREHOUSE
1340 E Hastings St
Downtown Eastside ⑤
+1 604 253 3022
gourmetwarehouse.ca

This 19.000-square-foot (1765-square-metre) warehouse is full of specialty ingredients and cookware essentials. The team travels the world over for authentic and original products before they hit the main markets. Appealing to professionals and home cooks, the staff are incredibly knowledgeable. If there's something you're on the hunt for, this is where you'll find it.

5 tempting
SPECIALTY ITEM SHOPS

101 **BETA5**
CHOCOLATE
409 Industrial Ave
Strathcona ⑤
+1 604 669 3336
shop.beta5chocolates.com

Named one of North America's top 10 chocolatiers, BETA5 melds art and science to produce chocolate both stunning in taste and appearance. BETA5 refers to the 5-beta crystal structure, the most stable form of cacao butter crystallization. The team produces both classic and original flavours, like the Polygon Noodle Bar with real ramen noodles in it.

101 BETA5

102 ORGANIC OCEANS
FRESH SEAFOOD
1505 W 1st Avenue
Granville Island ⑦
+1 778 869 1901
organicoceans.com

It doesn't get much fresher than this! While most of their business now operates in Steveston Village, you can still find Carlos and Fryda selling fresh in-season seafood on Friday, Saturday and Sunday afternoons from their locker at the False Creek Fisherman's Wharf. You'll find them over in aisle B!

103 LES AMIS DU FROMAGE
CHEESE
843 E Hastings
Downtown Eastside ⑤
+1 604 253 4218
buycheese.com

Established in 1985 by mother-daughter duo Alice and Allison Spurrell, les amis du FROMAGE sells a carefully chosen selection of local and imported cheeses and accompaniments. Their expert staff will help you navigate their impressive inventory of over five hundred cheeses and your picks will be cut to order.

104 VANCOUVER OLIVE OIL COMPANY
OLIVE OIL
2571 W Broadway
Kitsilano ⑦
+1 604 737 7171
vooc.ca

Founded in 2011, this family-owned shop is both an olive oil tasting room and retail space. Visitors are able to sample and purchase extra virgin and flavoured olive oils as well as balsamic vinegars. In order to stay true to their 'fresh is best' philosophy, their oil selection switches twice a year based on hemisphere.

105 ANY GROCERY STORE
MAPLE SYRUP

You'll find maple syrup for sale in tourist shops sprinkled all over the city. Our recommendation? Skip the tourist joints and go straight to the nearest grocery store. The maple syrup in here is just as good and far more affordable. Head to the cookie aisle for maple cream cookies.

The 5 best places for
INDIAN FOOD

---

106 VIJ'S RESTAURANT
3106 Cambie St
Mount Pleasant ⑧
+1 604 736 6664
vijsrestaurant.ca

It's impossible to talk about Indian food in Vancouver without mentioning Vij's. Owner, operator, chef and mastermind Vikram Vij opened the restaurant in 1994 and is known for his creative and contemporary take on Indian cuisine. The Lamb Popsicles with the Fenugreek curry are a must-order!

107 SULA INDIAN RESTAURANT
1128 Commercial Dr
Commercial Drive ⑥
+1 604 215 1130
sulaindian restaurant.com

Since 2010 this Commercial Drive gem has been consistently winning awards for it's inspired menu and decor. Keeping to traditional Indian preparations, the herbs are fresh and the garam masalas are roasted and made in-house. Surrounded by plants and water features, you'll feel like you're dining in a beautiful garden.

108 HOUSE OF DOSAS

1391 Kingsway
Knight ⑥
+1 604 875 1283
houseofdosas-bc.ca

Located on the corner of Kingsway and Knight, this is a no-fuss eatery and your go-to for South Indian cuisine in the city. Their *dosas*, which are large rice batter crepes filled with a variety of masala spiced curries, are served with lentil soup. The service is excellent, the food is delicious, the portions are large and the menu is easy on the wallet.

109 ASHIANA TANDOORI

1440 Kingsway
Knight ⑥
+1 604 874 5060
ashianatandoori.com

For the last 30 years, owner, operator and chef Rick Takhar and his team have been employing an ancient cooking technique called Ayurvedic, which combines health helping herbs and authentic Indian cuisine. Every ingredient used is thoughtfully chosen and their are plenty of gluten-free and vegan options. Try the *guncha-o-bahar*, *bangara* chicken and the Peshwari naan!

110 INDIAN ROTI KITCHEN

2961 Cambie St
Fairview ⑦
+1 604 876 3767
indianrotikitchen.com

This snug and simple restaurant specializes in, you guessed it, roti. The Indian-style flatbread wraps come stuffed generously with the veggie or meat filling of your choosing. Favourite options include the *paneer tikka*, *aloo gobi*, lamb *korma* and of course, the butter chicken.

5

HOLE IN THE WALLS

with excellent food

---

111 HAWKERS DELIGHT DELI

4127 Main St
Riley Park ⑨
+1 604 709 8188

This cash-only eatery is the epitome of a hole in the wall. Serving authentic Malaysian and Singaporean street food, the portions are large and the prices are cheap. Come here with friends and order to share. We recommend the spicy *mee pok*, the *mee goreng* noodles, the shrimp *laksa* and the addictive veggie fritters at the counter.

112 BON'S OFF BROADWAY

2451 Nanaimo St
Grandview-Woodland ⑥
+1 604 253 7242

Don't let Bon's rough-and-ready appearance scare you, this neighbourhood joint is known for its delicious comfort food including the fan favourite 2,95 dollar breakfast. The portion sizes are generous, the walls are covered in posters and autographs and the serve yourself coffee is bottomless. This is a good spot to remedy a hangover after a big night out.

113 THE LION'S DEN CAFE

615 E 15th Avenue
Mount Pleasant ⑧
+1 604 873 4555

Located on the edge of Fraser and Kingsway, this East Van cafe's menu is a mix of Japanese, Jamaican and all day breakfast. Run by husband-and-wife duo Ken Brooks and Junko Tanabe, the food tastes home cooked, is affordable and comes out quick. The jerk chicken is an easy win.

114 WHAT'S UP? HOT DOG!

2481 E Hastings St
Hastings-Sunrise ⑥
+1 604 879 8364
whatsuphotdog.ca

What's up? Vegan pub fare is what's up! This East Van bar located on Hastings serves an entirely vegan menu complimented with cocktails and craft beer. Don't miss out on the spicy peanut cauliflower wings and the cheap beer. The space is quirky, with a pinball machine and a technicolour wall.

115 DUNBAR PIZZA AND INDIAN FOOD

3348 Dunbar St
Dunbar ⑦
+1 604 732 4999
*dunbarpizza
indianfood.com*

This casual cafe brings together two very different cuisines: Italian and Indian. In addition to pizza and pasta they offer a full menu of authentic Indian dishes including crispy *samosas* and the best butter chicken in town guaranteed. Opt for the best of both worlds and order the butter chicken pizza!

AGRO ROASTERS

75 PLACES
FOR A DRINK

5 great
BREWERIES

---

116 STORM BREWING

310 Commercial Dr
Commercial Drive ⑥
+1 604 255 9119
stormbrewing.org

This is Vancouver's longest running craft brewery and a must-visit. Since 1994, brewer James Walton and the team have built a reputation for creating some of the most innovative and creative beers out there, including Apple Pie Ale and Whiskey Sour Pilsner. The garage-style brewery is not a tasting room; however, you can taste six 1oz samples.

117 STRANGE FELLOWS BREWING CO.

1345 Clarke Drive
Strathcona ⑤
+1 604 215 0092
strangefellows
brewing.com

Lovers of tradition and the West Coast, Strange Fellows brews some serious good beers. The brewery is handsome, with sleek and simple decor, and most importantly eight beers on tap. To pair they offer a small selection of local grub. Alongside the Tasting Room you'll find the Charles Clark Gallery, rotating artwork monthly.

118 RED TRUCK BEER COMPANY

295 E 1st Avenue
Strathcona (5)
+1 604 682 4733
redtruckbeer.com

After outgrowing their space in North Van, Red Truck made the move to its 34.000-square-foot (3159-square-metre) Brewery Creek location in 2015. Built on the values of a simpler time, the brewery is predominantly known for its lager and amber ale, which pair perfectly with their unreal burgers and hot dogs at the Truck Stop Diner.

119 STRATHCONA BEER COMPANY

895 E Hastings St
Downtown Eastside (5)
+1 778 379 9050
strathconabeer.com

Opened in 2016, this 25-hectolitre brewhouse uses fresh, high-quality ingredients and offers a type for every pallet. The modern, industrial-style tasting room has up to 12 rotating beers on tap, ready to fill flights, glasses and growlers. Their house-made pizza is always a good pairing choice.

120 OFF THE RAIL BREWING CO.

1351 Adanac St
Grandview-
Woodland (6)
+1 604 563 5767
offtherailbrewing.com

This East Van brewery loves English ales, German lagers and American IPAs, so naturally that makes up the majority of what they brew. Head upstairs to the bright and cozy tasting room where they have 15 beers on tap, including 3 nitro taps, which pour beer rarely available outside of the brewery.

The 5 most
UNUSUAL PLACES
FOR A DRINK

---

121 **THE SHAMEFUL TIKI ROOM**

4362 Main St
Riley Park ⑨
+1 604 999 5684
shamefultikiroom.com

From the outside, the blacked out windows block any indication of the tropical paradise that lies within. The Shameful Tiki Room is a homage to the outrageous tiki era that once was. The decor is authentic, draping the space in palms, wicker and warm lighting. The drinks are right on theme, one even being served to the sound of a gong.

122 **KEY PARTY**

2303 Main St
Mount Pleasant ⑧
+1 604 708 0881
keyparty.ca

Enter the Zottenberg & Sons Accounting office, pass the desk and knock on the door. Quickly, it will be answered and you will be invited to cross the threshold into this cheeky, 1970s themed bar. The cocktails have a whimsical throwback feel, like the Coconut Cream Grasshopper.

123 **HAIL MARY'S**

670 E Broadway
Mount Pleasant ⑧
+1 604 829 7032
hailmarys.net

With a cocktail for every deadly sin, Hail Mary's is for sinners. Drinks include The Holy Grail sangria and Penance, a vodka and Aperol mix. The decor is decidedly Catholic, with depictions of Mary and Jesus throughout. Going to the bathroom will literally take you to hell and back.

124 THE KEEFER BAR

135 Keefer St
Chinatown ⑤
+1 604 688 1961
thekeeferbar.com

Inspired by its Chinatown location and the apothecary's of old, you'll enter this moody cocktail bar under a sign that reads 'Medical Centre'. The menu, entitled 'List of Cures and Remedies', offers herb-infused drinks inspired by traditional Chinese medicine, created to soothe ailments and balance one's mood.

125 STORM CROW TAVERN

1305 Commercial Dr
Commercial Drive ⑥
+1 604 566 9669
stormcrow.com

This is the city's original nerd bar. What's a nerd bar? A sports bar for geeks, here card, board and role playing games are encouraged. The decor is fandom everything. Book your own private Dungeon Master and roll the twenty-sided shot dice at the bar. Check out Storm Crow Alehouse on Broadway for more nerdy fun.

125 STORM CROW TAVERN

5 hotspots for
COCKTAILS

―――――――

126 THE DIAMOND

6 Powell St
Gastown ①
di6mond.com

Overlooking Maple Tree Square in the historic Gastown, The Diamond is almost hiding in plain site. Whether it's a classic old-fashioned or a specialty cocktail from their rotating menu, every drink is expertly crafted. This cocktail bar is cool and laidback with an old soul, playing only vinyl music Thursday through Sunday.

127 UPSTAIRS AT CAMPAGNOLO

1020 Main St
Strathcona ⑤
+1 604 484 6018
campagnolo
restaurant.ca

Behind an unassuming green door and tucked above the restaurant Campagnolo is this relaxed full service cocktail lounge. They offer an impressive and thoughtful selection of wine and cocktails, and a small and limited supply food menu. If the Dirty Burger is still available, get your order in right away as it regularly sells out.

128 BOTANIST

1038 Canada Place
Coal Harbour ③
+1 604 695 5500
botanistrestaurant.com

This sophisticated and whimsical restaurant and bar is located in the Fairmont Pacific Rim. The drinks, developed by award-winning Creative Beverage Director Grant Sceney, are beautiful works of art and keep to the botany theme. The menu is split into five categories: Herb + Spice, Orchard + Field, Fruits + Vegetables, Flowers + Trees and the Cocktail Lab.

129 POURHOUSE RESTAURANT

162 Water St
Gastown ①
+1 604 568 7022
pourhousevancouver.com

The Pourhouse has an old-fashioned soul. Located inside a 100-year-old building, the interior has antique finishings and a 38-foot bar handcrafted from 120-year-old reclaimed Douglas fir. The cocktails are whiskey focused and include both simple and more complicated concoctions. The wine list is inspired and the beer selection is satisfying.

130 CLOUGH CLUB

212 Abbott St
Gastown ①
+1 604 558 1581
donnellygroup.ca/
clough-club

Named after John Clough, Vancouver's one and only lamplighter, this Gastown bar menu includes one-of-a-kind cocktails, 12 taps of Pacific Northwest beer and a 100% VQA-approved wine list. The interior, designed by Vancouverite Craig Stanghetta, has an old-timey flair paying homage to the historic neighbourhood in which it resides.

5 *lovely*
PATIOS

---

131 **MAHONY AT FALSE CREEK**

601 Stamps Landing
Fairview ⑦
+1 604 876 0234
discovermahony.com

On a good day this is probably the most sundrenched patio in the city. Located in the marina at the Stamps Landing, the large wrap-around deck has incredible views of False Creek. Like all good Irish pubs, they have a solid drink list and a tasty selection of grub. Don't forget your sunscreen!

132 **BRIX & MORTAR**

1138 Homer St
Yaletown ②
+1 604 915 9463
brixandmortar.ca

This chic dining house is located inside a 1912 Yaletown heritage building. The restaurant has two rooms, both beautiful, but the one we're here to talk about is the Homer Street room. The iconic glass covered outdoor courtyard patio has vines growing up the walls and a chandelier, it's truly an urban oasis.

133 THE NARROW LOUNGE

1898 Main St
Mount Pleasant ⑧
+1 778 737 5206
narrowlounge.com

This is about as hidden secret as it gets. Located on the corner of Main Street and 3rd Avenue, once you get there, look for the red light and go through the door. Even more unknown than The Narrow Lounge is their cute, tiki-esque patio, which is open through the warmer months.

134 THE ARBOR RESTAURANT

3941 Main St
Riley Park ⑨
+1 604 620 3256
thearborrestaurant.ca

You'll come here for the vegetarian comfort food, specifically The Classic Arburger, but you'll stay for the patio. Hidden behind the main restaurant, this is the perfect spot to take in brunch and happy hour. It's got cute furniture, heaters and lights on a string... What more does one need?

135 CARDERO'S RESTAURANT

1583 Coal Harbour Quay
Coal Harbour ③
+1 604 669 7666
vancouverdine.com/ carderos

Located in the Coal Harbour Marina, it doesn't get much more oceanfront than Cardero's. The interior is covered in warm wood and large windows. The patio is on the westside with views of Stanley Park and the beautiful marina They host live music every night from 8.30 pm, and also 3 to 6 pm every weekend.

5 expert
WINE BARS

136 **GRAPES & SODA**
1541 W 6th Avenue
South Granville ⑦
+1 604 336 2456
grapesandsoda.com

Vancouver's first natural wine bar (wine with little chemical and technological intervention) is situated right next door to its sister restaurant, the acclaimed Farmer's Apprentice. The interior is cozy and romantic, with bottles lining the wall and a small menu serving fresh, local bites.

137 **JUICE BAR**
54 Alexander St
Gastown ①
juicebaryvr.com

During the day this space doubles as The Birds and the Beets cafe, another wonderful Gastown spot. However, after hours Wednesday through Saturday it becomes a buzzy, intimate wine bar. They serve an always changing selection of natural wine paired with a carefully crafted menu from the resident chef.

138 **SALT TASTING ROOM**
45 Blood Alley Sq
Gastown ①
+1 604 633 1912
salttastingroom.com

Tucked down the cobblestoned Blood Alley, Salt Tasting Room specializes in artisan cheese, small-batch cured meats, and a dynamic wine list. Build your own tasting plate or go with the 'daily plate', either way gets paired with a wine flight picked to match. The interior has a long communal table and bottles lining the wall.

139 V.V TAPAS LOUNGE

957 E Hastings St
Downtown Eastside ⑤
+1 604 336 9244
vvtapaslounge.com

Situated in Strathcona Village, V.V Tapas Lounge delivers beautifully made small plates with local and international wines, craft beers and cocktails. The knowledgeable staff will help you make your pairing selections. We love this spot for its welcoming but refined ambience and charcuterie options.

140 THE STABLE HOUSE BISTRO

1520 W 13th Avenue
South Granville ⑦
+1 604 736 1520
thestablehouse.ca

This South Granville spot is on a mission to make wine more approachable. They offer an impressive wine list and selection of flight options, curated by top sommelier Matthew Landry. The intimate 36-seat bistro has a minimal but chic interior with white-washed panel walls, warm decor and a beautiful bar.

139 V.V TAPAS LOUNGE

5 wonderful spots to get your
COFFEE FIX

---

141 **AGRO ROASTERS**
550 Clark Drive
Grandview-
Woodland ⑥
+1 778 654 5727
agroroasters.com

Off the beaten track, this is a locally owned and operated, organic coffee roaster. The beans are carefully selected by the Head Roasters, including one of Canada's few licensed Q Graders (basically a sommelier for coffee). Agro has a keen interest in how and where coffee is grown. The cafe itself has an industrial interior, bright white and minimal.

141 AGRO ROASTERS

142 OLIVE + RUBY

2389 W Broadway
Kitsilano ⑦
+1 604 801 9600
oliveandrubycafe.com

Serving health-conscious fare and well-brewed bean water, Olive + Ruby serves espresso from Pallet Coffee Roasters, an amazing local roastery. The cafe is small, bright and quirky, covered in planters and natural wood. Grab a coffee and take a seat in one of their beautiful hanging chairs.

143 COFFEE ROASTERY MODUS

112 W Broadway
Mount Pleasant ⑧
+1 604 873 5111
moduscoffee.com

Opening the coffee shop in 2017, after a couple of years as an established roastery, Modus pushes the boundaries when it comes to their brew. Keeping it on the lighter side, they love a balanced and sweet coffee. The space is minimal, flooded with natural light, a handful of tables and a large communal bench.

144 KAHVE

1822 W 1st Avenue
Kitsilano ⑦
+1 604 222 9002
kahvevancouver.com

Serving up some of the best latte art in the city, this Kitsilano coffee shop offers smooth espresso drinks, a careful selection of food and the best London Fog in the city. The contemporary interior looks like a cross between an upscale boutique and a coffee shop with coffee related equipment and housewares on display.

145 MOVING COFFEE ROASTERY

64 E 3rd Avenue
Mount Pleasant ⑧
movingcoffee.com

Hidden inside Fife Bakery, this teeny tiny coffee shop is more like a coffee counter but let's be clear, that is no reflection of how good their coffee is. Run by husband-and-wife duo, Shirley and Edmond (a Q Grader), everything from a classic pour-over to their Morning Whiskey cold brew and sausage rolls is extraordinary.

The 5 best places for a
FUN NIGHT OUT

---

146 THE BELMONT BAR
   654 Nelson St
   Downtown ②
   +1 604 605 4340
   belmontbar.com

This newly renovated boutique hotel is broken down into four rooms: The Den and The Kitchen, which can be privately booked, The Living Room, a full service chill lounge, and The Basement, the place to party. Here you'll find an indoor bowling alley, lots of neon lights, rosé popsicles and good vibes.

147 COLONY
   965 Granville St
   Downtown ②
   +1 604 685 3288
   colonybars.com

This 15.000-square-foot (1393-square-metre) multi-level bar is located on the Granville Strip. Inside you'll find fifteen big screen TVs, an arcade featuring new and retro games, an indoor bocce court and three bars to grab drinks. This is a great spot to have a beer, a burger and some good times.

148 THE ROXY
   932 Granville St
   Downtown ②
   +1 604 331 7999
   roxyvan.com

It's practically a right of passage for Vancouverites, you've had at least one wild night at The Roxy. An institution of the Granville Strip, the Roxy has three bars, a large stage and live music every night. It's a reliable spot for a good night out.

149 HELLO GOODBYE

1120 Hamilton St
Yaletown ②
+1 604 669 6292
hellogoodbyebar.com

To get to this basement bar you'll pass through an unmarked door and down a hidden stairwell. This easy-to-miss 'drinking den' is an intimate, cozy haunt with dim lighting and a touch of artistic flair. The bar menu includes some finely crafted cocktails and DJs keep the party going late.

150 THE PORTSIDE

7 Alexander St
Gastown ①
+1 604 559 6333
theportsidepub.com

This Gastown bar is equal parts chill and equal parts party, with inspiration coming from the East Coast maritime pub culture. The interior is nautically themed with wood-lined walls, an upper deck which looks down onto the crowd below, two bars, a large dance floor and fairy lights hung overhead.

The LOCALS'
5 favourite spots for a drink

---

151 **ST. AUGUSTINE'S**
   2360 Commercial Dr
   Commercial Drive ⑥
   +1 604 569 1911
   staugustines
   vancouver.com

Named after the patron saint of beer, St. Augustine's has over 60 beers on tap ranging from a standard lager to a Root Beer Milk Porter. The beers all come from top-notch small breweries and the laidback restaurant serves typical gastropub food to pair. Check out their website for a live beer menu.

154 FINFOLK

152 THE BOXCAR

917 Main St
Strathcona ⑤
+1 604 398 4010
thecobalt.ca/the-boxer

If you don't know it's there this teeny-tiny pub is easy to miss. Essentially a narrow hallway, the Boxcar bar serves rotating craft beer taps and creative cocktails. Due to its size it can be tough to snag a seat, but if you can, you're in for an intimate and comfortable drink.

153 ALIBI ROOM

157 Alexander St
Gastown ②
+1 604 623 3383
alibi.ca

The Alibi Room is a local favourite for after-work beers and weekend sessions. The 'modern tavern' is located on the edge of Gastown inside a heritage building. They have fifty local and imported craft beers on tap, serve a menu of locally sourced food and the interior is very industrial-chic.

154 FINFOLK

1600 Franklin St
Grandview-
Woodland ⑥
+1 604 620 4935
finfolk.ca

This is a Scandinavian-inspired eatery in the heart of the East Van brewery district. Serving craft beer from breweries outside of the neighbourhood, it gives patrons a chance to try some of B.C.'s best craft beer without having to go very far. This hygge-ful joint also serves Scandi-Northwest bites, pizza and oysters.

155 SING SING

2718 Main St
Mount Pleasant ⑧
+1 604 336 9556
singsingyvr.com

Three words to describe Sing Sing? Beer, pho and pizza. The pho's are from passed-down traditional family recipes, the pizzas are creative and with twenty beers on tap, you'll find just what you're craving. The decor is easy on the eyes, bright with lots of natural wood and light, and greenery.

The 5 best places for
BUBBLE TEA

---

156 DRAGON BALL TEA HOUSE
1007 W King Edward Avenue
South Cambie
+1 604 738 3198

Located in South Cambie, this spot is a favourite amongst bubble tea lovers in Vancouver. It's unassuming, cash-only and has an extensive menu, which includes Asian flavours like red bean and matcha. There's only one location but don't be surprised if you start seeing these cups around town.

157 TAAN CHAR
7908 Granville St
Marpole ⑫
+1 604 428 8292

Known for their fruit teas, this Marpole bubble tea stop is a must. Opting to use fresh fruit as opposed to the more commonly used powder, the teas here are addicting and flavourful. Our favourite? The grapefruit. Hands down. For the adventurous, check out their cheese teas.

158 THE BUBBLE TEA SHOP
1680 Robson St
West End ③
+1 604 559 8208

New to bubble tea? Terrible at deciding? This is the bubble tea cafe for you! With cups split into two sections, you have an option to pick two different flavours here. The interior is cute with a small section of retail goods. Pair your drink with one of their delicious bubble waffles.

159 INFINI TEA

686 Seymour St
Downtown ②
+1 604 559 7639
infini-tea.business.site

This is the spot if you love your fruit tea made with real tea leaves. Not only does Infini Tea use whole loose leaves, they also use real fruit. The drinks are beautiful, they'll adjust the sugar and ice to your preference and the cafe is small, but clean and bright.

160 CATORO CAFE

666 E Broadway
Mount Pleasant ⑧
+1 604 423 2987
catorocafe.com

We might not have picked this one just for it's delicious bubble teas. Catoro is a Totoro-themed cat cafe. The space is separated into two areas, the cafe and the Cat Forest, which is home to a handful of feline friends that are up for adoption. There is a fee to enter the forest and weekends get busy so book ahead!

159 INFINI TEA

5 COFFEE SHOPS
worth a visit IN GASTOWN

---

161 REVOLVER
325 Cambie St
Gastown ①
+1 604 558 4444
revolvercoffee.ca

This is arguably Vancouver's favourite coffee shop. They boast an impressive bean selection from which you can pick and decide how you'd like it prepared. The industrial-chic interior space is very 'Gastown' and the coffee cake is the best in the city.

162 MILANO ESPRESSO LOUNGE
36 Powell St
Gastown ①
+1 604 558 0999
milanocoffee.ca

Founded by master roaster Brian Turko, the espresso drinks at Milano are smooth as can be, rich and just the right temperature. The staff are incredibly friendly and the interior is much larger than it looks on the outside, with lots of seating and space to get some work done.

163 NEMESIS COFFEE
302 W Hastings St
Gastown ①
nemesis.coffee

A visit to Nemesis is well worth walking the extra block or two from central Gastown. Coffee here is taken very seriously and the cafe is large, full of natural light, light wood and spilling hanging plants. The small menu and selection of snacks are about as good as the coffee. Order a pour-over or velvety espresso drink.

164 TIMBERTRAIN COFFEE ROASTERS

311 W Cordova St
Gastown ①
+1 604 915 9188
*timbertrain
coffeeroasters.com*

Around the block from the Gastown crowds is where you'll find this slice of caffeinated heaven. The drinks are all good here but the standout is their nitro cold brew, it's rich and refreshing. Think the Guinness of the coffee world. The interior is in line with the Gastown uniform.

165 CAFFÈ DI BEPPE

2 W Cordova St
Gastown ①
+1 604 564 6599
caffedibeppe.com

A nice break from the urban Gastown style, Caffè di Beppe is a Vancouver take on an old-school 'Italian caffe'. The 'Real Mocha' is our favourite item on the menu, with a sprinkle of cocoa on top, it is a must for any chocolate lover. The bar serves a selection of Italian pastries and deli items.

165 CAFFÈ DI BEPPE

5 welcoming places to
GRAB A HEALTHY DRINK

166 HEIRLOOM JUICE CO.

2861 Granville St
Fairview ⑦
+1 604 730 0022
heirloomveg.ca

Located just around the corner from its popular sister restaurant Heirloom is Heirloom Juice Co. Complimenting the food and drinks served at the eatery, the menu includes vegan juices, smoothies, salads, soups, and healthy snacks. Take something to go or take a seat and watch the bustle of South Granville.

167 MELU JUICE & HEALTH BAR

1110 W Pender St
Coal Harbour ③
+1 778 379 6358
melujuice.com

Using a hydraulic cold-press juicer to prevent any loss of nutrients and enzymes, MELU makes all of their products in-house with fresh and natural ingredients. In addition to the innovative beverages, the hip juicery also offer vegan nut mylks, meals and desserts.

168 THE JUICE TRUCK

4236 Main St
Riley Park ⑨
+1 604 620 6768
thejuicetruck.ca

The Juice Truck started out as, you guessed it, a food truck. After rising to success, they now operate four bricks and mortars in addition to their cart, our favourite location being the one on Main Street. Loved because they are so good, you'll find a varied menu of cold-pressed juices, smoothies and vegan bites.

169 SEJUICED VANCOUVER

1958 W 4th Avenue
Kitsilano ⑦
+1 604 730 9906
sejuicedvancouver.com

Located in Kitsilano, in addition to being one of the oldest juice bars in the city, it's also a much loved vegetarian eatery. Everything here has a homecooked feel, making for a comfortable clean-eating experience. The juice menu is broken down into Basics, Vital Fluids, Energy Elixers, Super Powershakes and Shots.

170 GLORY JUICE CO.

2186 W 4th Avenue
Kitsilano ⑦
+1 778 379 4511
gloryjuiceco.com

Created by a group of health-passionate friends, Glory Juice is another Vancouver success story. With four hip and modern locations around town, they deliver some of the best raw, 100% organic juices you'll ever get your hands on. Their popular juice cleanses come in three different types at 1-, 3-, 5-and 7-day lengths.

168 THE JUICE TRUCK

5 amazing ROOFTOPS
TO HAVE A DRINK

171 REFLECTIONS: THE GARDEN TERRACE

801 W Georgia St
Downtown ②
+1 604 673 7043
rosewoodhotels.com

Located in the inner courtyard on the fourth floor of the Rosewood Hotel Georgia you'll find The Garden Terrace. This elegant space serves light appetizers but is mostly known for their beautiful cocktails. We recommend their signature drink, the Hotel Georgia. Winter time? Have no fear, the terrace turns into a winter wonderland.

172 THE KEG STEAKHOUSE + BAR

1011 Mainland St
Yaletown ②
+1 604 633 2534
kegsteakhouse.com

Situated in the heart of Yaletown, this Keg location has one of the most desirable rooftop patios in the city. Keep your eyes peeled while you're here, it's a popular spot for celebrity watching, especially Canuck players. The lively patio can be enjoyed year-round as it is heated through the winter.

173 JOE FORTES SEAFOOD & CHOP HOUSE

777 Thurlow St
West End ③
+1 604 669 1940
joefortes.ca

This garden rooftop patio belongs to a Vancouver favourite. The relaxing patio has a living green wall, cozy outdoor fireplace, and a bustling horseshoe-shaped bar. Patio aside, the atmosphere and happy hour, which runs from 4 pm to 6 pm, are also good reasons to make a visit.

174 LIFT BAR & GRILL

333 Menchion Mews
Coal Harbour ③
+1 604 689 5438
liftbarandgrill.com

The view from this rooftop patio is breathtaking. On the water in Coal Harbour, there is nothing blocking your view of Stanley Park and the North Shore Mountains. The bi-level patio has plenty of seating and the restaurant serves sushi, steak, seafood and a good atmosphere.

175 DARBY'S PUBLIC HOUSE

2001 Macdonald St
Kitsilano ⑦
+1 604 731 0617
darbys.pub

More relaxed than the other locations on this list, Darby's has been a mainstay of the Kits community for 37 years. This neighbourhood spot has one of the largest rooftop patios with beautiful views of the North Shore and is a great spot to grab a beer with friends... they have over thirty on tap!

5 fun bars
TO CATCH A GAME

---

176 **THE CHARLES BAR**

136 W Cordova St
Gastown ①
+1 604 568 8040
thecharlesbar.ca

Occupying the ground floor of the famous Woodward's building, this is a modern but friendly sports bar. Built in a V-shape, the bar features an impressive nine-foot HD screen. In addition to a good selection of beers on tap, they have an equally good selection of well-crafted cocktails and food.

177 **THE PINT**
PUBLIC HOUSE

455 Abbott St
Gastown ①
+1 604 684 0258
vancouver.thepint.ca

With two floors, four bars and over eighty TVs, no matter what game or fight you want to watch, rest assured it will be playing here. Open from 11 am to 2 am, this is a great place to settle in for a day of watching sports. The Pint does get pretty lively after sunset, especially once an event at one of the stadiums finishes.

178 RED RACER TAPHOUSE

871 Beatty St
Yaletown ②
+1 778 379 2489
redracertaphouse.com

With its roots as a suburb brewpub, Red Racer has grown into one of the best places to catch a game in the downtown core. There are plenty of TVs, a huge rotating selection of seasonal beers (40 of which are on tap) and far better than average pub food coming from the kitchen, all making for a fun atmosphere.

179 SHARK CLUB SPORTS BAR & GRILL

180 W Georgia St
Downtown ②
+1 604 687 4275
sharkclub.com

With over 60 TVs, plenty of beer on tap and good pub grub, catching a game at the Shark Club is a no-brainer. Located just a couple blocks from our main stadiums, Rogers Area and BC Place, this places fills up with sports fans before, during and after events nearby.

180 CRAFT BEER MARKET

85 W 1st Avenue
Mount Pleasant ⑧
+1 604 709 2337
craftbeermarket.ca

With a large selection of brews and several big screens scattered around the beer hall, CRAFT is definitely at the top of our list for game-worthy spots in Vancouver. Occupying the entirety of the historic Salt Building, the space is massive, meaning there is plenty of room for you and your crew to hang out.

5 *places to drink an amazing*
CAESAR

---

181 EDIBLE CANADA

1596 Johnston St
Granville Island ⑦
+1 604 682 6681
ediblecanada.com

The Caesar is Canada's unofficial national drink and this Canadian bistro has one of the best in the city. In fact, their Maple Bacon Caesar might be the most Canadian drink around. The cocktail features dill and horseradish infused Stealth vodka, lime juice, Clamato, Tabasco and Worcestershire..

182 TUC CRAFT KITCHEN

60 W Cordova St
Gastown ①
+1 604 559 8999
tuccraftkitchen.com

The signature Caesar at this farm-to-table favourite includes Montelobos mezcal, Espolòn Reposado tequila, Walter Craft Caesar Mix and tomato shrub (tomatoes, fire-roasted jalapeños, spices and apple cider vinegar). Finished with dashes of Tabasco and Addition Thai Green Chili bitters.

183 THE LOCAL

2210 Cornwall Ave
Kitsilano ⑦
+1 604 734 3589
localkits.com

Across the street from Kits Beach, a Caesar at The Local is the perfect way to kick off the day before spending it in the sun. Served in their signature boot glass, the El Caesar is a combo of Smirnoff vodka, Mott's Clamato Juice, special Mexican hot sauce and a pepperoni stick.

184 CHEWIES OYSTER BAR

1055 W Hastings St
Coal Harbour ③
+1 604 620 7634
chewies.ca

Known for their oysters and New Orleans-inspired fare, Chewies also mixes up a mean Caesar. Their rendition is comprised of New Amsterdam vodka, fresh horseradish, Clamato, and their top-secret blend of spices. It's garnished with a Cajun prawn and Kevin's bacon. Not feeling the vodka? Swap it for Bulleit bourbon, Tanqueray gin, or Olmeca Altos tequila instead.

185 SCORE ON DAVIE

1262 Davie St
West End ③
+1 604 632 1646
scoreondavie.com

You can't talk about Caesars in Vancouver without mentioning Score. They feature a number of them on their menu, the most-talked about being the 60 dollar Checkmate Caesar, which is piled high with onion rings, a burger, a hotdog and other fried goodies. These folks take the garnish game to a whole other level.

182 TUC CRAFT KITCHEN

5 first-class
MICRODISTILLERIES

---

186 LONG TABLE DISTILLERY

1451 Hornby St
Downtown ②
+1 604 266 0177
longtabledistillery.com

Established in 2010, this is Vancouver's first microdistillery. Head Distiller and co-owner Charles Tremewen and his team have produced award-winning, small-batch gin and seasonal spirits, distilled from 100% Canadian grain spirits. The ingredients used are organic, handpicked by expert foragers inspiring their West Coast flavours.

·187 THE LIBERTY DISTILLERY

187 THE LIBERTY DISTILLERY

1494 Old Bridge St
Granville Island ⑦
+1 604 558 1998
thelibertydistillery.com

Lovers of tradition and truth, The Liberty Distillery produces top of the line handcrafted spirits, specifically whiskey, unaged whiskey, gin and vodka. Stop by The Liberty Distillery Lounge any day of the week for signature cocktails in their 110-year-old antique tasting room or join them on the weekend for distillery tours.

188 ODD SOCIETY SPIRITS

1725 Powell St
Grandview-
Woodland ⑥
+1 604 559 6745
oddsocietyspirits.com

This East Van distillery is dedicated to combining Old World traditions with experimentation. Under the stewardship of founder and Master Distiller Gordon Glanz, the team here are not afraid of the unknown. The tasting lounge is refined but welcoming, with a touch of otherworldly.

189 ARTISAN SAKEMAKER

1339 Railspur Alley
Granville Island ⑦
+1 604 685 7253
artisansakemaker.com

Built on three key objectives: sustainable, natural and local, Artisan SakeMaker has been producing award-winning, small-batch sake under their brand name 'OSAKE' since 2007. In 2015 the winery reached a milestone, officially producing all their products from 100% Canadian ingredients. If you're curious about the sake-making process, book a winery tour.

190 RESURRECTION SPIRITS

1672 Franklin St
Grandview-
Woodland ⑥
+1 604 253 0059
resurrectionspirits.ca

These guys are the cool kids of the local microdistillery scene. They use locally sourced grain, botanicals and spices, and their batches are seriously small. For example, there are only 350 bottles of their Rosé Gin, which is casked in cabernet sauvignon barrels for 6 months.

HEY JUDE SHOP

75 PLACES TO SHOP

———

5 top-notch
SPECIALTY SHOPS

191 THE MODERN BARTENDER

28 E Pender St
Chinatown ②
+1 604 684 1747
themodernbartender.com

Tucked away in Chinatown, The Modern Bartender has anything and everything for the bar enthusiast. With a selection of over 200 types of bitters, glassware for everything and gadgets galore, the interior has a mystical apothecary feel.

192 PAPER-YA

1666 Johnston St, #9
Granville Island ⑦
+1 604 684 2531
paper-ya.com

Ya means store in Japanese, and quite simply Paper-Ya is just that, a paper store. Located in the heart of Granville Island, the shop is best known for the beautiful handmade paper they import from all over the world. It doesn't stop there though, Paper-Ya features a wide selection of complementary merchandise.

193 GRANVILLE ISLAND BROOM CO.

1406 Old Bridge St
Granville Island ⑦
+1 855 519 0506
broomcompany.com

Owners Mary and Sarah Schwieger say it often, no two brooms from the Granville Island Broom Co. are the same. Handcrafted in Vancouver using antique tools and equipment, the brooms are all made in the Shaker style originating in the eastern United States. Using quality materials, the brooms are long lasting and functional.

194 BUTTON BUTTON

318 Homer St, #202
Gastown ①
+1 604 687 0067
buttonbutton.ca

As you might have guessed, this small Gastown shop is lined floor to ceiling, wall to wall with buttons. With inventory from all over the world, made from every material imaginable and in every colour possible, owner Angela Ho will be happy to help you find just the button you're looking for.

195 BEADWORKS

1666 Johnston St, #5
Granville Island ⑦
+1 604 682 2323
beadworks.ca

Family-owned and -operated since 1986, if it has to do with beads, BeadWorks has you covered. This one-of-kind shop is full to the brim with beads of all colours, sizes and shapes. Make your own jewellery in store! Grab a design tray and make your selections. A staff member will help you put it all together – it makes for a one of a kind souvenir!

193 GRANVILLE ISLAND BROOM CO.

5 *unique*
SECONDHAND SHOPS

196 **VALUE VILLAGE**
1820 E Hastings St
Grandview-
Woodland ⑥
+1 604 254 4282
stores.savers.com

For those who aren't afraid to put in work, you'll get the most bang for your buck here. Being the closest to downtown and most central location of the popular secondhand chain means you're bound to strike gold with top brands and quality goods. New product is put out daily so there's always fresh merchandise to sort through.

199 HUNTER & HARE

197 COMMUNITY THRIFT & VINTAGE

11 W Hastings St
Gastown ①
+1 604 629 8396
*communitythrift
andvintage.com*

Opening in 2011, this thrift shop doubles as a social enterprise. Selling a 'tightly edited collection' of preloved fashion, including some unreal vintage tees, Community Thrift supports at-risk people through their compassionate work training program and donate profits to the PHS Community Services Society.

198 MINTAGE MALL

245 E Broadway
Mount Pleasant ⑧
+1 604 428 6732
*mintage-mall.
business.site*

If you're looking for real-deal vintage goods and not just secondhand items get yourself to Mintage Mall. Within the 'mall' you'll find individually curated rooms, each one associated with different sellers and their own shops. The items are carefully handselected ensuring quality and authenticity.

199 HUNTER & HARE

227 Union St
Chinatown ⑤
+1 604 559 0282
hunterandhare.com

Find clothes that fit your style without spending a fortune. This women's consignment shop showcases in-season, preloved apparel and accessories. The shop itself is adorable and well organized, making shopping easy and fun. The green faux-moss wall highlights the local and favourite vendor products they also sell.

200 THE MAIN EXCHANGE

3728 Main St
Riley Park ⑨
+1 604 708 1009
themainexchange.ca

Miranda Dendewich-Mizrahi opened The Main Exchange in 2014 at just 24 years old. The cute boutique is a women's consignment shop, carrying a good selection of in-season styles. Miranda and her staff are so incredibly friendly and will be quick to help find just what you're after.

5 elegant
FASHION SHOPS
FOR WOMEN

201 THE LATEST SCOOP

305 Water St
Gastown ①
+1 604 428 5777
thelatestscoop.ca

With its roots as a summertime pop-up shop, Vancouverites love this boutique for being on trend and affordable. The goal of The Latest Scoop is to make you fall in love with your wardrobe over and over again. The broad selection offers everything from classic tees to printed outerwear. If you're on the hunt for a cute dress this should be your first stop!

202 HEY JUDE SHOP

315 Abbott St
Gastown ①
+1 778 836 4694
heyjudeshop.com

With contemporary style in mind, founders Lauren Clark and Lyndsey Chow prove season after season that recycled clothing can look beautiful and be on trend. With a focus on clean silhouettes and natural fibres and featuring a small sampling of like-minded brands, the vintage clothing shop is a little slice of curated heaven.

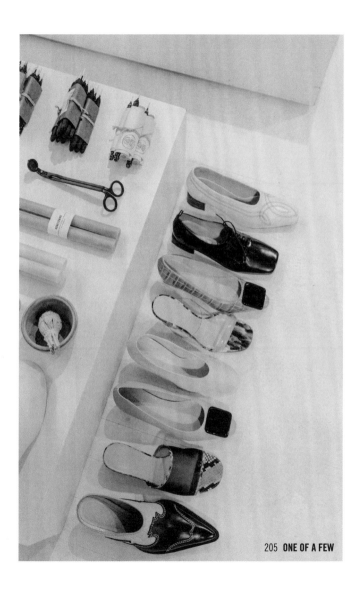

203 NETTLE'S TALE

330 W Cordova St
Gastown ①
+1 604 633 8907
nettlestale.com

Founder Julia Church decided enough was enough and after a successful crowdfunding campaign launched Nettle's Tale, an inclusive swimwear line. The brand has grown tremendously and has since opened a lifestyle shop carrying not only Nettle's Tale suits but also a selection of ethically made and thoughtfully sourced clothes and accessories, the epitome of feel good fashion.

204 WOO TO SEE YOU

3671 Main St
Riley Park ⑨
+1 604 874 3622
wootoseeyou.com

Woo To See You buys with a developed style in mind, meaning if you like one thing at the shop, you will probably like it all. The shop buys in small amounts and because of this has new things hitting the racks frequently. On top of the clothes, they feature a small selection of complementary accessories and goods.

205 ONE OF A FEW

353 Water St
Gastown ①
+1 604 605 0685
oneofafew.com

Established in 2005, this small but beautifully curated shop finds some of the best pieces from creatives all over the world and brings them right to Gastown. Offering a selection of clothing, footwear, accessories and objects, this is the shop for those who appreciate artistry and see apparel as art waiting to be worn.

5 stylish
FASHION SHOPS
FOR MEN

---

206 FILSON

47 Water St
Gastown ①
+1 604 689 1836
filson.com/
vancouver-store

While the headquarters are just south of the border in Seattle, Filson in Gastown is just too cool of a shop not to mention. Renowned for making products from near indestructible materials, the company is all about creating functional products at the highest quality – perfect for life in the great white north.

207 RODEN GRAY

8 Water St
Gastown ①
+1 604 689 7302
rodengray.com

Specializing in men's on-trend streetwear, Roden Gray takes the best of the best from international designer labels and showcases them in the Gastown shop. The space is minimal and masculine with two floors, clean lines and exposed brick and pipes.

208 THE CORNER STORE

2601 Main St
Mount Pleasant ⑧
+1 604 602 1668
cornerstore
vancouver.com

Previously in Gastown under the name 'Complex', The Corner Store made the move to its current location on Main Street nearly ten years ago. A staple of the streetwear scene in Vancouver, the men's apparel shop continues to be a pioneer carrying a super curated selection of brands and collections. Their sneaker selection also happens to be one of the hottest in the city.

209 WALLACE MERCANTILE SHOP

253 Columbia St
Gastown ①
+1 604 620 0211
wallacemercantil
shop.com

With authenticity at its core, this shop is all about finding clothes that can keep up with an active day but also transition well into a fine evening. They have an eye for streamlined design, high-quality materials and always think about function. The decor is simple but thoughtful, just like their products.

210 NEIGHBOUR

12 Water St, #125
Gastown ①
+1 604 558 2555
shopneighbour.com

Neighbour is one of those stores you could spend a long time just standing in, wishing you could live there. A Vancouver original, Neighbour leans towards quality over quantity and trends. The shop also carries a selection of items, objects and books that reflect the persona of the good neighbour the shop models itself after – one that is honest, listens well and is quick to help.

The 5 best
BOUTIQUES FOR BOTH

211 8TH & MAIN

2403 Main St
Mount Pleasant ⑧
+1 604 559 5927
8main.ca

Settling on the name 8th & Main after they were unable to agree on anything else, this shop is named after the intersection in Mount Pleasant it sits on the corner of. The boutique is one of the largest shops on the street, carrying a wide selection of both large and small brands for both men and women at reasonable prices.

215 THE BLOCK

212 FRONT & COMPANY

3772 Main St
Riley Park ⑨
+1 604 879 8431
frontandcompany.com

Known for their extravagant window displays, Front first opened its doors on Main Street in 1993 selling consignment clothes, antiques and vintage jewellery. The shop is split into three separate spaces; the gift shop, the pop-up-shop space and the main retail space filled with consignment and new contemporary apparel.

213 ROWAN SKY

334 W Cordova St
Gastown ①
+1 604 568 2075
rowansky.com

While there are no clothes here, if you're looking for footwear and accessories, Rowan Sky has you covered. Owners Troy Cruickshank and Nima Farahmand opened the boutique in 2009 and have a sharp eye in choosing beautifully designed high-quality products. Regularly picking up new brands, they often carry labels found nowhere else in the city.

214 STILL LIFE

2315 Main St
Mount Pleasant ⑧
+1 604 876 5659
stilllifeboutique.com

Established in 1984 in Victoria, owners Matt and Kim purchased Still Life in 2007 and opened the Vancouver location in 2013. The beautiful, airy shop carries contemporary, casual apparel for men and women by international designers. The staff are friendly and quick to help.

215 THE BLOCK

350 W Cordova St
Gastown ①
+1 604 685 8885
theblock.ca

Carrying a mix of popular and hard-to-find brands, The Block has established itself as a go-to shop for men and women's apparel. The space has high ceilings, worn concrete floors and an impressive built-in accessory wall. With an emphasis on independent designers, they have lots of unique pieces.

5 inspiring
INTERIOR DESIGN
SHOPS

216 L'ATELIER HOME

425 W Cordova St
Gastown ①
+1 604 684 9933
latelierhome.com

Sourcing products from all over the
world, L'Atelier HOME is a standout
amongst the Gastown design stores.
The neutral tones of the shop and
showroom are bright and inviting no
matter how grey the day is. The decor
is minimal but the fabrics and textures
bring it to life and feel rich.

217 THE CROSS DECOR & DESIGN

1198 Homer St
Yaletown ②
+1 604 689 2900
thecrossdesign.com

Opening in 2003, few people do 'pretty'
better than the team at The Cross. Inside
the Yaletown shop you'll find 8500 square
feet (790 square metres) of exposed brick
and beautifully curated decor. The store
describes their style as "a little bit beachy,
a little bit romantic, and very West Coast".

220 **OLD FAITHFUL SHOP**

218 PARLIAMENT INTERIORS

115 Water St
Gastown ①
+1 604 689 0800
parliamentinteriors.com

Specializing in space-saving furniture for small spaces, Parliament Interiors is a must-stop for those looking for something to freshen up a space. The furniture and decor are crisp, modern and functional with mid-century modern design elements. The colour palette can be described as white and grey with hits of 'it' colours. Check out the Kermodi Living Art section for some stunning interior plants.

219 PROVIDE

1805 Fir St
South Granville ⑦
+1 604 632 0095
providehome.com

Opened in 2007, Provide founders Robert Quinnell and David Keeler opened the interior design store to showcase the treasures they found while travelling the world. With an eye for the sublime, the duo continue to travel, on the hunt for the soulful, well-crafted decor to feature in their beautiful location, just off of South Granville.

220 OLD FAITHFUL SHOP

320 W Cordova St
Gastown ①
+1 778 327 9376
oldfaithfulshop.com

A new take on the old-school general store, Old Faithful Shop carries quality goods for simple, everyday living. With incredible service, the shop is tucked inside a historic Gastown building built in 1903. Inside the exposed brick walls, the shop filled with products made to stand the test of time in both style and durability.

The 5 most tempting
BOOKSHOPS

221 MACLEOD'S BOOKS

455 W Pender St
Downtown ②
+1 604 681 7654
macleodsbooks.
tumblr.com

MacLeod's Books has been called one of
the last great bookshops. Selling books
for as much as 40.000 dollar and as little
as 1 dollar, stepping into the bookstore
is like stepping into a labyrinth. It's
a complete mix of madness and magic,
that only the staff seem to understand.
Prepare yourself to be awed.

222 THE PAPER HOUND

344 W Pender St
Downtown ②
+1 604 428 1344
paperhound.ca

Co-owners and bibliophiles Rod Clarke
and Kim Koch have both been buying and
selling books since they were teenagers.
Together they opened The Paper Hound,
a new, used and rare bookstore located
right downtown. Carrying all genres,
the bookstore has impressive philosophy
and poetry sections. The shop is cozy,
warmly lit and often has old-timey music
playing overhead.

223 TANGLEWOOD BOOKS

2306 W Broadway
Kitsilano ⑦
+1 604 736 8876
tanglewoodbooks.ca

Tanglewood Books in Kitsilano has been helping Vancouverites find the perfect book since 1993. Specializing in buying and selling top-quality used, out of print and rare books, the shop carries everything from absolute classics to bestsellers. The shelves are tall and the space is well organized, making it easy and fun to browse.

↑ 222 THE PAPER HOUND

224 BANYEN BOOKS AND SOUND

3608 W 4th Avenue
Kitsilano ⑦
+1 604 732 7912
banyen.com

This is Canada's most comprehensive metaphysical bookstore, selling a wide variety of books and resources on spirituality, health and earth wisdom traditions. Opening in 1970, Banyen is always evolving and describes itself as "an oasis, a crossroads, a meeting place for East and West…". Welcoming love and wisdom, here you'll find information on everything from acupuncture and Zen to celestial spheres.

225 MASSY BOOKS

229 E Georgia St
Chinatown ⑤
+1 604 721 4405
massybooks.com

This funky and vibrant bookshop located in Chinatown is nothing but welcoming. The 1500-square-foot (140-square-metre) space has floor-to-ceiling bookshelves filled with books of every genre, perfect for browsing. The shelves are regularly pushed aside to host readings and events. Don't forget to take a peek upstairs at the 400-square-foot (37-square-metre) art gallery, showcasing local emerging artists.

5 original
GIFT SHOPS

226 **GIVING GIFTS**

4570 Main St
Riley Park ⑨
+1 604 831 7780
givinggifts.ca

With room after room filled with locally made, fair trade and eco-friendly products, you're bound to find the perfect little something in this Main Street shop. Their commitment on giving doesn't stop there though, the boutique gift shop is known for giving back to the artists they work with and the community they operate in.

227 **BIRD ON A WIRE CREATIONS**

2535 Main St
Mount Pleasant ⑧
+1 604 315 1188
birdonawire creations.com

Supporting local artists and artisans, Bird on a Wire Creations curates some of the city's best one-of-a-kind objects. Selling only handmade creations, the product range is endless ensuring you'll find that perfect something for that special someone. Bird on a Wire is on a mission to help make the shift from 'starving artists' to 'thriving artists'.

228 NINETEEN TEN

4366 Main St
Riley Park ⑨
+1 604 558 0210
nineteenten.ca

Offering a wide selection of well-made goods, this bright and beautiful boutique is a one-stop-shop for gifts. With an emphasis on independent and Canadian made goods, the shop offers a wide variety of curated products including stationary, textiles, apothecary and home goods. Not only will you find the perfect gift, but likely something for yourself as well!

229 FAR OUT COFFEE POST

2173 Dundas St
Grandview-
Woodland ⑥
+1 604 875 8090

There are so many reasons to love this little East Van outpost – it's got great coffee, delicious food, plenty of plants, old-school pinball machines and of course, awesome vintage finds. Scour the racks of tees, Levis and patterned button-ups with one of the best Americanos in the city in hand.

230 BAMBOO VILLAGE

135 E Pender St
Chinatown ⑤
+1 604 662 3300
bamboovillage.
weebly.com

This family-run business has been operating in historic Chinatown for over 35 years. In addition to offering a wide selection of bamboo products, the shop carries an incredible range of Chinese goods including lanterns, one-of-a-kind oriental furniture, houseware and gifts. Shopping here is always a unique experience... you'll never know what you're going to find!

5 not-to-miss
RECORD STORES

---

231 NEPTOON RECORDS

3561 Main St
Riley Park ⑨
+1 604 324 1229
neptoon.com

Opened in 1981 by father-son duo Rob and Ben Frith, Neptoon is Vancouver's oldest independent record shop. Inside the bright green building, the store is filled with albums meticulously organized. Not only does Neptoon buy and sell vinyl but also host intimate gigs and produce a lot of local talent under the shop's record label.

232 BEAT STREET RECORDS

439 W Hastings St
Gastown ①
+1 604 683 3344
beatstreet.ca

Opened in 1996 by co-founders Avi Shack and Wes Kuitenbrouwer, Beat Street was originally a skateboarding and apparel shop. It quickly transitioned into a record store and was a hot spot for DJs in the 1990s and 2000s. The shop has an urban vibe and roughly 50.000 records in stock.

233 ZULU RECORDS

1972 W 4th Avenue
Kitsilano ⑦
+1 604 738 3232
zulurecords.com

A finalist on nationwide search for the best record shop, Zulu Records is one of the most well known record stores in the country. The shop has a huge inventory of new and used vinyl and CD's and sells turntables and vintage gear as well. Regularly hosting artists from all over the world, the shop is a West 4th institution.

234 AUDIOPILE

2016 Commercial Dr
Commercial Drive ⑥
+1 604 253 7453
audiopile.ca

East Van's go-to record shop, Audiopile opened its doors in 2001. Hipster heaven, the shop has a huge inventory of new and used LPs, CDs and cassettes. The staff are knowledgeable and passionate, be sure to check out the Staff Picks section if you're looking to find your next favourite album.

235 DANDELION RECORDS & EMPORIUM

2442 Main St
Mount Pleasant ⑧
+1 778 737 7367
dandelionemporium.
blogspot.com

Stepping into Dandelion Emporium it becomes clear quickly that Jeff Knowlton and Laura Frederick, the husband-and-wife team behind the shop, have a background in design. The vinyl inventory is carefully selected and they offer some impressive specialties including psych and krautrock. Along with the records, you'll also find a selection of curated art, books and jewellery.

231 NEPTOON RECORDS

5 *expert*
TATTOO PARLOURS

---

236 LIQUID AMBER TATTOO & ART COLLECTIVE

62 Powell St
Gastown ①
+1 604 738 3667
liquidambertattoo.com

Located in a three-story heritage building in the heart of Gastown, Liquid Amber has been providing custom and cosmetic tattoos to patrons since 2001. With a nearly all-female staff, the atmosphere of the shop is warm, welcoming those from all walks of life. On the walls you'll find a curated gallery featuring the work of local artists.

237 GASTOWN TATTOO PARLOUR

105 W Cordova St
Gastown ①
+1 604 642 6556
gastowntattoo.com

Perhaps the most buzz worthy tattoo parlour in the city, Gastown Tattoo maintains an impressive fifteen artist roster including some of the most in demand in the city. The shop has an old-school vibe but with new-school standards, with lime green walls and quirky animal heads and art covering the walls.

238 EAST VAN INC

1839 Commercial Dr
Commercial Drive ⑥
+1 604 299 3939
eastvaninc.com

Welcoming newcomers and tattoo enthusiasts, East Van Inc located on Commercial Drive is known for their custom tattoos, piercings and of course, the neon East Van cross sign. The iconic sign is a landmark of the neighbourhood and the shop sells a line of inspired merchandise. The artists at the shop are some of the best in the bizz.

239 BLACK MEDICINE TATTOO

119 E Pender St
Chinatown ⑤
+1 778 379 9975

Tucked in between two Chinese bulk-food stores, you might miss Black Medicine the first time you walk past. The shop is well known online for their minimalist tattoos they turn out, but if that's not your style have no fear. They have a roster full of talented artists for all types of ink.

240 ADRENALINE-GRANVILLE

1014 Granville St
Downtown ②
+1 604 669 6800
adrenalinestudios.com

With two shops in the city, one downtown and the other in Kitsilano, no matter the style you're looking for, Adrenaline has the artist for you. Known Canada wide as a premier tattoo parlour, the shops have high standards and produce some of the best ink to be found walking around the city.

5 great
SPORTSWEAR SHOPS

241 RYU APPAREL

1745 W 4th Avenue
South Granville ⑦
+1 604 428 6778
ryu.com

Standing for 'Respect Your Universe', RYU focuses on urban athletic apparel; tough enough for the hardest workouts but still fits with your life outside of the gym. The Vancouver based company recently opened locations in the United States but their flagship bricks and mortar on West 4th Avenue carries the widest selection and is a thing of beauty.

242 VANCOUVER RUNNING CO

1886 W 1st Avenue
Kitsilano ⑦
+1 778 379 8511
vanrunco.com

As the name suggests, Vancouver Running Co has you covered for all your running needs. Home to what might be the most beautiful shoe wall in the city, the displays look minimalist but the high-end apparel and accessories are not. The shop carries the latest and greatest in running gear from all over the world and supports both road and trail running.

243 LADYSPORT

3545 W 4th Avenue
Kitsilano ⑦
+1 604 733 1173
ladysport.ca

Carrying one of Canada's largest selection of athletic footwear, LadySport is the one-stop-shop for women's athletic wear in the city. Since 1983, the knowledgeable staff has been helping shoppers find not only the right product but the right fit as well. This is the place to go for the sports bra you've been on the hunt for!

244 LULULEMON LAB

50 Powell St
Gastown ①
+1 604 689 8013
shop.lululemon.com

While there are many Lululemon stores all over town, there is only one Lululemon Lab. The lab is a design concept space offering focused collections specific to Vancouver, including both athletic and street wear. The shop has an in-house team of designers and limited quantities of each exclusive lab item are produced.

245 PUBLIC MYTH

1631 Powell St
Grandview-
Woodland ⑥
+1 604 737 8565
publicmyth.com

Public Myth has a passion for the planet and the people who love it. This Vancouver company prides itself on choosing natural and sustainable materials, as well as producing their products ethically, with most of it manufactured in the city. The East Van showroom carries their full collection of women's workout and casual apparel.

The 5 cutest
FLOWER SHOPS

246 **THE WILD BUNCH**
1525 West 6th Ave
South Granville ⑦
+1 604 423 4399
thewildbunch.ca

Known for the natural look and feel of their arrangements, The Wild Bunch aren't shy about their love of flowers. The talented team focuses on using seasonal blooms and foliage, sourcing locally whenever possible. Their beautiful working studio is open to the public Monday through Saturday, they also host regular workshops.

246 THE WILD BUNCH

247 BLOSSOM & VINE FLORAL CO.

156 E 11th Avenue
Mount Pleasant ⑧
+1 604 428 2004
blossomandvine
floralco.com

This florist suits its cozy Mount Pleasant location perfectly. The shop has an old-fashioned feel, and is irresistibly Instagram-able. The blooms and bouquets are stunning and if you don't see what you're looking for, owner and designer Michelle will help you make it.

248 OUR LITTLE FLOWER COMPANY
AT: GRANVILLE ISLAND MARKET

1689 Johnston St, #505
Granville Island ⑤
+1 604 633 0283
olfco.ca

Located in the busy Granville Island Market, cousins Erin and Kerstyn opened this location in 2016. The aromas of the blooms can be smelt even over the market, indicating just how fresh the flowers are. Sourced from local and imported growers, a beautiful arrangement is the perfect finish to your market shopping.

249 CELSIA FLORAL

1930 Arbutus St
Kitsilano ⑦
+1 604 731 3314
celsiaflorist.com

This boutique flower shop is known for the signature style and artistry. The lovely brick-front shop is inside a Kitsilano heritage home with an adorable arched entryway. Inside the space is quaint, filled with fresh flowers, whimsical ready-to-go bouquets and a wide selection of plants.

250 LEIS DE BUDS

2202 W 4th Avenue
Kitsilano ⑦
+1 604 428-7858
leisdebuds.com

It's impossible to walk past Leis de Buds without a 'wow-ing' at the impressive blooms and plants spilling out of the shop. Step inside and soak it all up while swinging away on one of the indoor swings! They are also known for their sustainable and eco-friendly business model.

5 VANCOUVER MUST-HAVES

251 HERSCHEL BACKPACK

herschel.ca

Founded in 2009 and based in Vancouver, you'd be hard-pressed to go a couple of blocks without seeing someone with a Herschel backpack. Known for their simple silhouettes and technical features, the brand has done some impressive collaborations, has a popular kids line and has recently broken into the apparel market. Check out their flagship store in Gastown for the widest selection.

252 LULULEMONS

shop.lululemon.com

Once you notice the subtle Lululemon logo, you'll start seeing it everywhere and on everyone. Founded in 1998 by Vancouverite Chip Wilson, Lululemon is a yoga-inspired athletic apparel brand. With close to 15 stores in the Lower Mainland alone, they are known for their quality products and design and inspiring manifesto. A pair of Lulu leggings is a staple in the Vancouverite wardrobe.

253 ARC'TERYX JACKET

arcteryx.com

Established in 1989 in North Vancouver, Arc'teryx is a high-end sporting goods company known for producing the best quality products on the market. Living in a rainforest means Vancouverites are serious about their rain jackets and despite their impressive price tag, Arc'teryx jackets are worn all around town. The global headquarters is still in North Van and the manufacturing facility is in New Westminster.

254 VANCITY SWEATSHIRT

vancityoriginal.com

Vancouver is a laidback, casual city which means wearing a sweatshirt around town is totally acceptable. The brand behind the popular VANCITY logo, The Vancity Original Brand, was established in 1998 by Mister Martini, a co-owner of one of the first hip-hop clubs in Canada. The simple red, white and black phrase, is found most commonly on sweatshirts, hats and shirts, is popular with locals and visitors to the city.

255 REUSABLE CUP

Vancouverites are notorious for being an environmentally conscious group and big users of reusable cups. To encourage the reduction of waste coffee shops offer discounts to those who bring their own mug. The second reason a Vancouverites love their reusable cups is a little bit sneaky… Drinking alcohol is prohibited in the city's parks and beaches. We'll let you make the connection there.

The 5 best places to buy beautiful
FIRST NATIONS ART
and JEWELLERY

---

256 HILL'S NATIVE ART

120 E Broadway
Mount Pleasant ⑧
+1 604 685 4249
hills.ca

This impressive 4000-square-foot (372-square-metre) Mount Pleasant gallery is home to one of the largest collections of Northwest Coast Native Art. Featuring over 1200 Native artists and representing every Nation of the Northwest Coast, you'll find everything here from totem poles to rattles and drums.

257 COASTAL PEOPLES FINE ARTS GALLERY

332 Water St, #200
Gastown ①
+1 604 684 9222
coastalpeoples.com

Perhaps Vancouver's most famous destination for First Nations art, the Coastal Peoples Gallery showcases museum quality artwork. The pieces are handcrafted by emerging and established aboriginal artists from the Pacific Northwest Coast. New exhibits open every year featuring a wide selection of pieces including masks, glasswork and their specialty, custom wedding bands.

260 **LATTIMER GALLERY**

258 FAZAKAS GALLERY

688 E Hastings St
Railtown ⑤
+1 604 876 2729
fazakasgallery.com

Located in East Van, this commercial gallery and exhibition space features a diverse offering of contemporary Northwest Coast indigenous art. Director LaTiesha Fazakas honed her skills as a curator while simultaneously working as an art dealer and completing her Art History degree at UBC. The gallery is bright and ever-changing.

259 INUIT GALLERY OF VANCOUVER

206 Cambie St
Gastown ①
+1 604 688 7323
inuit.com

Established in 1979, this Gastown gallery includes not only Northwest Coast artwork but also Inuit. Featuring high-quality works from senior and up-and-coming artists, the collection includes a wide variety of pieces but has a particularly good selection of sculptures and graphics.

260 LATTIMER GALLERY

1590 W 2nd Avenue
South Granville ⑦
+1 604 732 4556
lattimergallery.com

After spending much of their adult lives travelling B.C. and establishing strong relationships with indigenous artists, husband-and-wife Leona and David Lattimer opened their gallery in 1986. The space is warm and inviting, inspired by the Northwest Longhouse, and includes an impressive display of jewellery, carvings, sculptures, totem poles and much more.

The 5 best shops in
CHINATOWN

261 **NEW TOWN BAKERY & RESTAURANT**
148 E Pender St
Chinatown ⑤
+1 604 689 7835
newtownbakery.ca

This casual counter service eatery has been serving the best of Filipino and Chinese baked goods since 1980. Their apple tarts are award-winning, their steamed buns are Vancouver famous (order the *asado*) and the egg tarts are delicious. Everything is baked fresh every day!

262 **BEIJING TRADING CO LTD.**
89 E Pender St
Chinatown ②
+1 604 684 3563

The walls of this traditional Chinese apothecary are lined with jars full of exotic herbs and remedies, including rare wild ginseng for energy and bird nests to help with indigestion. Not sure what you should buy? There's a traditional pharmacist on site that will help you find the right remedy.

263 **THE CHINESE TEA SHOP**
101 E Pender St
Chinatown ②
+1 604 633 1322
thechineseteashop.com

Despite its size, this tiny corner shop stocks an impressive selection of rare and exotic teas. However even more impressive is the owner and tea master Daniel Liu's knowledge of his inventory and craft. For a nominal price he will take you step-by-step through the elaborate Chinese tea ceremony, which includes multiple samples.

264 AI & OM

129 E Pender St
Chinatown ②
+1 604 428 8784
aiandomknives.com

Founded by Douglas Change, Ai & Om Knives is a Japanese knife shop located in the heart of Chinatown. With years of experience working with top chefs, all the knives and knife accessories in the shop are carefully selected with both the professional and amateur in mind. Douglas and the Ai & Om team are incredibly passionate, knowledgeable and quick to help.

265 MING WO COOKWARE

23 E Pender St
Chinatown ②
+1 604 683 7268
mingwo.com

While there's no food sold here, Ming Wo has been a cornerstone of the Chinatown culinary community for over 100 years. Established in 1917, they carry the best inventory of professional cookware around. The friendly and incredibly knowledgeable staff will help you find just what you're looking for... even if you don't know exactly what that is.

261 NEW TOWN BAKERY & RESTAURANT

MARINE BUILDING

20 BUILDINGS TO ADMIRE

The 5 most
UNIQUE EXAMPLES
OF ARCHITECTURE

---

266 **DR. SUN YAT-SEN CLASSICAL CHINESE GARDEN**

578 Carrall St
Chinatown ②
+1 604 662 3207
vancouver
chinesegarden.com

Opened in 1986, the Dr. Sun Yat-Sen Classical Chinese Garden is the first Chinese garden built outside of China with the goal being to 'maintain and enhance the cross-cultural understanding'. Employing the philosophical principles of feng shui and Taoism, the plants were chosen according to their blossom schedule in order to emphasize the changing seasons, especially the 'awakening spring'.

267 **VANCOUVER PUBLIC LIBRARY – CENTRAL BRANCH**

350 W Georgia St
Downtown ②
+1 604 331 3603
safdiearchitects.com

Completed in 1995, the Vancouver Public Library Central branch was designed by Moshe Safdie and after winning a design competition held by The City of Vancouver. The building's exterior with its enclosed, glass-roofed concourse, resembles the Roman Colosseum. Offering many public spaces, like the roof garden, the library reported an increase of 800.000 visitors the year following its completion.

268 THE MARINE BUILDING

355 Burrard St, #1000
Coal Harbour ③
+1 604 683 8604
vancouverarchitecture.
mikepriebe.ca

Completed in 1930, The Marine Building is widely considered the best example of architecture in the city and one of the finest art deco examples in the world. Designed by McCarter Nairne and Partners, the skyscraper stands at 97,8 metres and was the tallest building in the city until 1939. The project cost 2,3 million dollar but due to the Great Depression was sold to the Guinness family for 900.000 dollar. In 2016 its estimated value was 90 million dollar.

266 DR. SUN YAT-SEN CLASSICAL CHINESE GARDEN

269 THE QUBE

1333 W Georgia St
Coal Harbour ③

Winning the 1970-71 Design in Steel Award, architects William Rhone, Randle Iredale and structural engineer Bogue Babicki are the geniuses responsible for The Qube. Built in 1969 from the top down, construction of The Qube first began with the completion of its 13-story core. With the elevated first floor resting on a pedestal, despite its precarious shape, the building is one of the most earthquake-resistant structures in the city.

270 EUGENIA PLACE

1919 Beach Avenue
West End ③

With a 37-foot (11,28-metre) Pin Oak tree growing from the top and its unmistakable syringe-like shape, Eugenia Place is a standout structure. Designed by architect Richard Henriquez, who named it after his mother, there are many interpretations of the design; some believe it pays tribute to the height of the Douglas firs that stood there previously with the syringe and tree on top symbolizing injecting nature back into Mother Earth.

5 wonderful
BRIDGES

271 CAPILANO SUSPENSION BRIDGE

3735 Capilano Road
North Vancouver ⑲
+1 604 985 7474
capbridge.com

Originally built in 1889 by George Grant Mackay with cedar planks and hemp rope, the 140-metre-long 70-metre-high suspension bridge was completely rebuilt in 1956 into the wire cable style it is now. Keep your blood pumping by checking out the Treetops Adventure and the Cliffwalk. Canyon Lights, a beautiful winter lights festival, runs from mid November to the end of January.

272 LYNN CANYON SUSPENSION BRIDGE

3663 Park Road
North Vancouver ⑲
+1 604 990 3755
lynncanyon.ca

Standing 50 metres above a raging river, this lesser-known bridge opened to the public in 1912 and cost 10 cents to cross. Today the bridge is free and is a great alternative to those not up for paying the Capilano Suspension Bridge fee. The centre of the bridge offers impressive views of the canyon and the park is full of trails, waterfalls and swimming spots.

273 LIONS GATE BRIDGE

Lions Gate Bridge Rd
Stanley Park to
North Vancouver ④⑩

Officially known as the First Narrows Bridge, the Lions Gate Bridge is a suspension bridge crossing the First Narrows of the Burrard Inlet. Opened in 1939, Lions Gate refers to The Lions peaks of the North Shore Mountains. Prospect Point in Stanley Park offers good views of the bridge and aerial views of the Sea Wall can be found by walking its south side.

274 GRANVILLE STREET BRIDGE

Granville Island
to Yaletown ⑦②

Spanning False Creek, the Granville Street Bridge is one of the major thoroughfares connecting the peninsula of downtown. From above, the bridge provides a good look of downtown, the inlet and the other bridges. Better yet is the view of the bridge from Granville Island, which the bridge covers. From here you can see the belly of the beast and some hidden street art.

275 SKY PILOT SUSPENSION BRIDGE

36800 BC-99
Squamish ⑪
+1 604 892 2550
seatoskygondola.com

One of the many attractions found at the top of the Sea to Sky Gondola, the Sky Pilot Suspension Bridge has 360-degree views of Howe Sound, the Coastal Mountains and surrounding forests. Despite being at the top of a mountain, the 100-metre-long bridge is open year-round, so bring your snow boots in the winter!

273 LIONS GATE BRIDGE

5 *impressive*

HISTORIC BUILDINGS

---

276 HOTEL EUROPE

43 Powell St
Gastown ①

This six-story heritage building was designed by Parr and Fee Architects and built in 1909. Designed in the Flatiron style to fit the triangular lot, it was the first reinforced concrete structure built in Canada. The building can be seen in many films including *The Changeling* and *Legends of the Fall* and still has its original Italian tile floors and lead glass windows.

277 ROGERS SUGAR FACTORY

123 Rogers St
Downtown Eastside ②
+1 604 253 1131
lanticrogers.com

Dating back to 1890 when Vancouver was only four years old, the factory is the oldest industrial site in the city and has been integral to the local economy. The property, built along the Canadian Pacific Railway tracks, is 13,5 acres (54.632 square metres) and comprised of 20 buildings, including a couple built in 1940s art deco style. The factory still is a functioning refinery, producing almost 10% of Canada's sugar output.

278 THE SYLVIA HOTEL

1154 Gilford St
West End ③
+1 604 681 9321
sylviahotel.com

Designed as an apartment building by W.P. White, the building was constructed in 1912 for Mr. Goldstein, named after his daughter Sylvia. Following the Depression, the transition was made into full-service hotel. The hotel is known for the Virginia creeper vines that cover one side of the building and as the first pet-friendly hotel in the city; the resident cat Mr. Got To Go inspired three popular children's books by Lois Simmie.

279 HOLY ROSARY CATHEDRAL

646 Richards St
Downtown ②
+1 604 682 6774
holyrosarycathedral.org

Built in the French Gothic style, the cathedral first opened its doors in December 1900. The most prominent feature of the cathedral is its two asymmetric bell towers, which hold its eight bells. There are 21 stained-glass windows, the most notable being the five made by Canadian artist Guido Nincheri. The exterior walls are made of sandstone from Gabriola Island.

280 VANCOUVER ART GALLERY

750 Hornby St
Downtown ②
+1 604 662 4700
vanartgallery.bc.ca

Once the main courthouse for Vancouver until 1979, the building that now houses the Gallery was designed in 1905 by Francis Rattenbury, who also designed the B.C. Parliament Buildings. Named a National Historic Site of Canada, the neoclassical building features iconic columns, a central dome and ornate stonework. Due to its central location and large lawn, it is often used as a gathering spot for demonstrations and protests.

The 5 most
HIGH-END
NEIGHBOURHOODS

281 KITSILANO
Kitsilano ⑦

Known for its laidback, beachy vibes, Kitsilano is home to the most expensive dwelling in Vancouver. Built in 2008 and valued at 73,12 million dollar, the 15.694-square-foot (1458-square-metre) house is owned by Lululemon founder Chip Wilson. Spanning four waterfront lots, take a stroll past 3085 Point Grey Road for a closer look.

282 WEST POINT GREY
(See overview map)

This affluent neighbourhood includes Jericho and Spanish Banks beach parks, high-end boutiques, casual eateries and impressive mountain views. Tucked back a block from the beach is Belmont Avenue. This residential street includes five out of ten most expensive homes in the city, with an average price tag of 43 million dollar.

283 SHAUGHNESSY

(See overview map)

Established in 1907, this neighbourhood was developed by the Canadian Pacific Railway and was intended for the city's elite population. The most valuable home in the neighbourhood, located at 3489 Osler Street, has a price tag of 35,16 million dollar, is 17.000 square feet (1580 square metres) and includes an indoor pool, an underground garage and a 2000-square-foot (186-square-metre) maid's residence.

284 COAL HARBOUR

Coal Harbour ③

Unlike the other neighbourhoods on this list, the residencies in Coal Harbour are almost exclusively condos. This Downtown subsection neighbours the Financial District, the West End and Stanley Park. The most expensive condo, valued 32,34 million dollar, occupies the top floor of 277 Thurlow Street, is 8000 square feet (743 square metres) and has six bathrooms.

285 SOUTHLANDS

(See overview map)

Located in southwest Vancouver, this neighbourhood is known for its tree-lined streets and multimillion-dollar mansions on acreage. Described as a 'country urban neighbourhood' and a 'haven for horse lovers', the equestrian club is a community focal point. Valued at 22,19 million dollar, the most expensive dwelling sits on 4,2 acres (17.000 square metres).

SEAWALL

50 PLACES
TO DISCOVER

———

5 lovely
SEAWALL STOPS

286 **GIRL IN A WETSUIT**

2743 Stanley Park Dr
Stanley Park ④

Located on the northeastern section of the Seawall, *Girl in a Wetsuit* is a life-size bronze sculpture by Elek Imredy. There's some controversy over the piece as it closely resembles the *Little Mermaid* statue found in Copenhagen. On close inspection you can see the goggles on the girl's head and flippers on her feet.

287 **THE TEAHOUSE IN STANLEY PARK**

7501 Stanley Park Dr
Stanley Park ④
+1 604 669 3281
vancouverdine.com

The Teahouse in Stanley Park is towered by trees one side and has amazing views of the ocean and mountains on the other. While not quite fine dining, the restaurant is refined and romantic, serving brunch, lunch and dinner. This is a great spot to watch the sunset.

288 **SIWASH ROCK**

Stanley Park ④
vancouver.ca

The iconic Siwash Rock is the only sea stack for miles. This basalt rock exists due to a volcanic dike that formed in the sandstone and mudstone foundation, forcing hot magma up. According to the Squamish people's historical account, the rock is testament to a man named Sklash's dedication to fatherhood.

289 BROCKTON POINT LIGHTHOUSE

Stanley Park Road
Stanley Park ④
vancouver.ca

One of two lighthouses in Stanley Park, Brockton Point Lighthouse overlooks the Burrard Inlet. The first lighthouse was built in 1890 and had one keeper, Davy Jones, who is credited for saving many from drowning in the busy harbour. The current lighthouse was built in 1914 and runs automatically. Don't forget to look up! The lighthouse sits right above the Seawall path.

290 SECOND BEACH POOL

735 Stanley Park Dr
Stanley Park ④
+1 604 257 8371
vancouver.ca

After a long run, walk or ride on the Seawall, Second Beach Pool is always a good idea. The heated outdoor fresh-water pool is open May to September. With lifeguards on duty and two waterslides, it's a great spot for families. Additionally, there is a section for 50-metre lanes for those looking to get in some aquatic exercise.

289 BROCKTON POINT LIGHTHOUSE

5 highlights on the
SEA TO SKY highlights

291 PORTEAU COVE PROVINCIAL PARK

38 KM NORTH
OF VANCOUVER
Squamish-Lillooet ⑪
+1 604 986 9371
seatoskyparks.com

This popular stop is located on the shores of Howe Sound, the most southerly fjord in North America. The park is large, roughly 50 hectares and features shoreline spots for camping and picnicking. Scuba diving is very popular here with two sunken vessels and artificial reefs attracting lots of marine life.

292 TANTALUS RANGE LOOKOUT

Sea to Sky Highway
Squamish ⑪

A subrange of the Pacific Coast Mountains, the Tantalus Range is named after Mount Tantalus, the largest mountain amongst them. The viewpoint pullout and information hut are located on the south side of the highway. If you have the time, check out the Tantalus Range Lookout Trail located in Brohm Lake Forest close by. The 5-kilometre loop takes about 5 hours but offers amazing scenery.

293 BACKCOUNTRY BREWING

405-1201 Commercial Way
Squamish ⑪
+1 604 567 2739
backcountry brewing.com

Sometimes after a long hike or day on the road you just need a cold beer. The good news is, Backcountry Brewing has you covered. Established in 2017, the 6000-square-foot (557-square-metre) brewery and kitchen has a mid-70s ski cabin vibe, complete with shingles and vintage decor. Their Trailbreaker Pale Ale took home first place at the BC Beer Awards and third at the Canadian Brewing Awards.

294 THE WATERSHED GRILL

41101 Government Rd
Brackendale ⑪
+1 604 898 6665
thewatershedgrill.com

Nowhere captures the culture of Squamish better than the Watershed. From the outside the restaurant looks like a regular house but upon further inspection you'll find stunning views of the river and mountains and also the dining room, bar and patio. The atmosphere is chill, they use local and organic meat paired with local craft beers and regularly host live music.

295 BRANDYWINE FALLS

47 KM NORTH
OF SQUAMISH
Whistler ⑪
+1 604 986 9371
env.gov.bc.ca

This is a good stop to get out and stretch your legs before the final sprint to Whistler. The lesser-known Brandywine Falls is a spectacular 70-metre waterfall surrounded by crumbling caverns. The walk to the waterfall is about 15 minutes there and back across a covered footbridge and through forest.

5 delightful places to
WATCH THE SUNSET

296 LIGHTHOUSE PARK

4902 Beacon Lane
West Vancouver ⑩
+1 604 925 7275
westvancouver.ca

Everything from the first-growth Douglas fir forest to the rocky coastline of Lighthouse Park is beautiful. Once arriving at the National Historic Site, make your way to the West Beach Trail. This path will take you to one of the best vantage points in the park to watch the sunset. Don't forget your camera and a light to guide you back after the sun goes down.

296 LIGHTHOUSE PARK

297 SUNSET BEACH PARK

1204 Beach Avenue
West End ③
+1 604 873 7000
vancouver.ca

Aptly named, Sunset Beach is located downtown at the mouth of False Creek. This beach is smaller and quieter than it's neighbour English Bay, but is also close to amenities, cycling and walking paths and has logs on the sand to sit and lean against. This is a great spot to throw down a blanket and enjoy the end-of-day sun with friends.

298 PROSPECT POINT

5601 Stanley Park Dr
Stanley Park ④
+1 604 669 2737
prospectpoint.com

With the Lions Gate Bridge to the right, the North Shore Mountains straight ahead and the open ocean to the left, Prospect Point at sunset is a dream. Grab a coffee at the cafe and hang out until the bridge lights come on, adding more romance.

299 WHYTECLIFF PARK

7102 Marine Drive
West Vancouver ⑩
+1 604 925 7275
westvancouver.ca

One of the many gems of West Vancouver, this cliffside park offers spectacular views of Howe Sound any time of day, but especially at sunset. With the setting sun in the background, the mountains of the Gulf Islands and coastline create a beautifully layered gradient of colour.

300 THIRD BEACH

Near 7501 Stanley
Park Drive
Stanley Park ④

On sunny Tuesday nights from late spring to early fall, Third Beach turns into a bongo beach party! The informal drum circle begins midafternoon when the Brahm's Tams Drum Circle gathers on the beach. The event attracts fellow jammers and hundreds of listeners who take in the music and setting sun. The event is completely free.

5 important places to
EXPERIENCE HISTORY

301 MUSEUM OF VANCOUVER

1100 Chestnut St
Kitsilano ⑦
+1 604 736 4431
museumofvancouver.ca

Sharing an entrance and foyer with the H.R. MacMillan Space Centre in Vanier Park, the Museum of Vancouver is the oldest museum in the city and the largest civic museum in Canada. Founded in 1894, the award-winning museum showcases Vancouver-centric exhibitions discussing the city's past, present and future.

302 VANCOUVER POLICE MUSEUM

240 E Cordova St
Railtown ⑤
+1 604 665 3346
*vancouverpolice
museum.ca*

Opening in 1986 to commemorate the Vancouver Police Department's centennial, the museum houses over 20.000 objects including confiscated firearms and weapons, counterfeit currency, photographs, archived documents and other memorabilia. To add to the eeriness, the building was once the Coroner's Court and autopsy facilities. Be sure to join a 'Sins of the City' walking tour of the neighbourhood.

303 9 O'CLOCK GUN
Stanley Park Drive
Stanley Park ④

Cast in England in 1816 the 9 O'Clock Gun has helped Vancouverites keep time since it was brought to Stanley Park in 1895. Originally firing at 6 pm to signal the end of the fishing day, it later changed to 9 pm to ensure the public and ships kept accurate time. The 12-pound cannon now fires automatically and has a parody Twitter account.

304 GASSY JACK STATUE
1 Water St
Gastown ①

Born in Hull, England John 'Gassy Jack' Deighton came to B.C. in 1858 hoping to strike it rich in the Gold Rush. Finding no gold and after his original bar in New Westminster failed, Deighton opened a second bar called the Globe Saloon, where his statue now stands. Called 'Gassy Jack' for his love of storytelling, the area became known as Gastown.

305 TERRY FOX STATUE
855 Expo Boulevard
Downtown ①

Voted one of Canada's greatest Canadians, Terry Fox was an athlete, activist and Vancouverite. In 1977, at age 18, Terry was diagnosed with cancer and his leg was amputated. Three years later he began his 'Marathon of Hope' with the goal to run across Canada and raise money for cancer research. Averaging 42 km a day, sadly his journey ended in 143 days when it was discovered his cancer had spread. Terry died shortly after but Canadians still take part in Terry Fox Runs and over 715 million dollar has been raised in his name.

The 5 most memorable
CITY VIEWS

306 **QUEEN ELIZABETH PARK**

4600 Cambie St
Riley Park ⑨
+1 604 873 7000
vancouver.ca

The horticultural jewel of the city, at 152 metres above sea level this park is also the highest point making for amazing views of the city and North Shore Mountains. After checking out the view, tour the manicured gardens or pop into the Bloedel Conservatory, a beautiful indoor tropical garden.

307 **VANCOUVER LOOKOUT**

555 W Hastings St
Gastown ①
+1 604 689 0421
vancouverlookout.com

Situated in the Financial District of Downtown, inside the Harbour Centre, the Vancouver Lookout takes you up over 550 feet (167 metres) in 40 seconds to a viewing deck offering 360-degree views of the city. Another way to see the mountain and city views is to dine at the Top of Vancouver Revolving Restaurant.

308 **CYPRESS HIGHVIEW LOOKOUT**

Cypress Bowl Road
West Vancouver ⑩

This lookout is located just off the road on your way up to Cypress Mountain Resort. From here you'll see incredible views of the Lions Gate Bridge, Stanley Park, Burrard Inlet and the downtown. Best time to go is as the sun is setting, highlighting the city.

309 **CHARLESON PARK**

999 Charleson St
Fairview ⑦
+1 604 873 7000
covapp.vancouver.ca

Within this peaceful park you'll find winding paths, a waterfall and a pond. If you make your way towards the Seawall you'll also find a striking view of the downtown shoreline. In one shot you'll be able to see the gleaming glass buildings, boats moving through False Creek and people zipping along the Seawall opposite.

310 **SECRET CAMBIE CLIMBING TREE**

Cambie Corridor ⑨

Known as the Cambie Climbing Tree, this special spot offers one of the best views of the city but you have to find it first. The impressive evergreen features a hammock, tire swing and perfectly spaced branches. The location is kept secret via the honour system, however, if you head south from the King Edward SkyTrain Station you may just find it.

307 VANCOUVER LOOKOUT

The 5 most interesting
TOURS

311 **FORBIDDEN VANCOUVER WALKING TOURS**
207 W Hastings St
Gastown ①
+1 604 227 7570
forbiddenvancouver.com

Showcasing the Vancouver's unique history, Forbidden Vancouver takes people through the streets of the city highlighting some of the deepest and darkest moments of its past. There are five tour options: The Lost Souls of Gastown Tour, The Forbidden Vancouver Tour, The Dark Secrets of Stanley Park Tour, The Really Gay History Tour, and Art Deco & Chocolate Tasting Tour.

312 **HARBOUR AIR – THE MAIL RUN**
AT: UNIT #1 BURRARD LANDING
1055 Canada Place
Coal Harbour ③
+1 604 274 1277
harbourair.com/tours/ the-mail-run

Based on historical mail delivery routes, this seaplane tour departs from downtown and takes you harbour hopping through the Gulf Islands. You get the best of both worlds with panoramic views of the city, the mountains and the Strait of Georgia. The tour is customizable, with a three-hour option or full day with a stop on Salt Spring Island.

313 DEEP COVE KAYAK – FULL MOON TOUR

2156 Banbury Road,
Deep Cove
North Vancouver ⑩
+1 604 929 2268
deepcovekayak.com

See the Pacific Northwest coast in a whole new light… Moonlight to be precise! Deep Cove Kayak runs moonlight guided kayak tours two or three evenings closest to each full moon. Watch the moon rise over the eastern mountains and flood the Indian Arm with its light.

314 A WOK AROUND CHINATOWN

MEET AT:
578 Carrall St
Chinatown ②
+1 604 736 9508
awokaround.com

This is not your average food tour. Join off-duty chef Robert as he guides you through one of Vancouver's most vibrant neighbourhoods, Chinatown. You'll learn all about its culinary and cultural happenings, from historical landmarks to specialty shops featuring tea and crispy duck. You'll also enjoy some dim sum along the way.

315 CYPRESS TOUR – CHEESE & CHOCOLATE FONDUE TOUR

6000 Cypress Bowl Rd
North Vancouver ⑩
+1 604 922 0825
cypressmountain.com/
guided-snowshoe-
tours/chocolate-fondue

This tour is for lovers of cheese, chocolate and the great outdoors! You'll snap on your snowshoes and headlamp and follow your guide through the winter wonderland trails of Cypress Mountain. After working up an appetite, you'll finish at the ultra-cozy Hollyburn Lodge for cheese and chocolate fondue.

5

ON-SET SCENES

316 **DEADPOOL**

A twinned bridge, the Georgia Viaduct connects Downtown with Main Street and Strathcona. Despite being one of the most congested roads in the city, the Viaduct was shut down for two weeks in April 2016 to film a major fight scene in *Deadpool*, starred in and directed by Vancouver's own Ryan Reynolds.

317 **ELF**

Because this Christmas classic, *Elf*, is based in New York City, very little of the Vancouver skyline can be seen on screen. This being said, many of the indoor scenes were filmed in different locations around town. The Hudson's Bay Vancouver Downtown was used for the interior of the Gimbels department store where Buddy meets the fake Santa.

318 TWILIGHT

Scenes from all four movies in the series *Twilight* were filmed in and around Vancouver. You'll find the Cullen's house in West Vancouver, Jacob's house in Coquitlam, Bella cliff jumped in Whytecliff Park, Downtown doubled as Seattle and many of the dense mossy forest scenes were filmed in Golden Ears Provincial Park.

319 50 SHADES OF GREY

All of the movies in this franchise were filmed in and around Vancouver. In addition to the street scenes filmed in Gastown (specifically down Alexander Street), the Bentall 5 building was used for Grey Enterprises, UBC played Washington State University, the Fairmont Hotel Vancouver was used as the Heathman Hotel and Christian Grey ran around Coal Harbour.

320 X-MEN

X2, X-Men: The Last Stand and *X-Men Origins: Wolverine* were filmed in the Lower Mainland and on Vancouver Island. Locations include: Royal Roads University's Hatley Castle was used for Professor Xavier's School for Gifted Youngsters, Jean Grey's house is in Tsawwassen and Alouette Lake played the part of Alkali Lake where Phoenix rose from.

The 5 best spots to feel the
HOLIDAY SPIRIT

321 ROBSON SQUARE SKATING

800 Robson St
Downtown ②
+1 604 646 3554
robsonsquare.com

Robson Square rink is situated in the centre of downtown between the streets Robson, Georgia, Howe and Hornby. Skating at the open-air rink begins December 1st and runs until the end of February. Skating is free with your own skates, otherwise rentals cost 5 dollar a pair. Live music is regularly scheduled during the holiday season and there is a concession with warm drinks and snacks.

322 VANDUSEN FESTIVAL OF LIGHTS

5151 Oak St
Shaughnessy
+1 604 257 8335
vandusen.ticketzone.com

VanDusen Gardens is worth seeing anytime of the year but especially at Christmas. The annual Festival of Lights begins end of November and runs until the beginning of January. The display features over 1 million lights spread across 15 acres of gardens. The event attracts 110.000 per season so buy your tickets online to save money, skip the line and secure your spot.

323 VANCOUVER CHRISTMAS MARKET
AT: JACK POOLE PLAZA

1055 Canada Place
Coal Harbour ③
+1 778 200 0167
vancouverchristmas market.com

Located in Jack Poole Plaza, the Vancouver Christmas Market brings festive Old World traditions to our modern city. Modelled after authentic German Christmas markets, the event offers hut after hut of handcrafted artisanal treasures and tasty bites and sips, including mulled wine. There is live holiday music, a spot to see Santa and endless Yuletide sparkle.

324 CHRISTMAS AT CANADA PLACE

999 Canada Place
Coal Harbour ③
+1 604 665 9000
canadaplace.ca

For the month of December the Canadian Trail (west promenade) of Canada Place is illuminated with holiday displays and activities. Presented by the Port of Vancouver, the event has been happening for over 30 years. Major attractions include the 'Chrismoose', a 15-foot-tall moose light sculpture, the Avenue of Trees and the iconic Sails of Light.

325 SINGING CHRISTMAS TREE CONCERT
AT: BROADWAY CHURCH

2700 E Broadway
East Vancouver ⑫
+1 604 253 2700
singingchristmastree.org

Since 1967 thousands have made their way to Broadway Church to participate in the Singing Christmas Tree Concert. The free event takes place 10 times over the holiday season. While it isn't the only Christmas concert in Vancouver, it's likely the most impressive. The stage features a giant Christmas tree with 10 levels, from which the over-80-member choir performs.

The 5 nicest
CITY BEACHES

---

326 ENGLISH BAY BEACH
Beach Avenue
West End ③

Located in the West End neighbourhood of downtown, English Bay is the city's most popular beach for sun lovers and swimmers. Also called First Beach, the horizon view looks out onto the busy Burrard Inlet, dotted with big and small boats. The beach is also the location of many Vancouver events, including the Celebration of Lights fireworks competition and the New Year's Day polar bear swim.

327 KITSILANO BEACH
1499 Arbutus St
Kitsilano ⑦
vancouver.ca

Known for its stunning beauty and wide range of facilities, a sunny day in Vancouver means a busy day at Kits Beach. The beach boasts soft white sand, volleyball courts, tennis courts, concessions, restaurants, a playground and a small grass field. Additionally, Kits Pool is Canada's longest pool at 137 metre and is Vancouver's only outdoor heated salt-water pool.

328 AMBLESIDE BEACH

Argyle Avenue
West Vancouver ⑩
vancouvers
northshore.com

Across the Burrard Inlet from downtown is West Vancouver's most popular beach, Ambleside Beach. The Centennial Seawalk, a 1,7-km trail that runs along and past the beach, has scenic views of the Inlet, the Coast Mountains, the Vancouver skyline and ships travelling under the Lions Gate Bridge.

329 SPANISH BANKS

4875 NW Marine Dr
West Point Grey
vancouver.ca

Further removed than many of the other city beaches means that Spanish Banks is often less busy. While technically it is just one bank, the beach is split into three sections: Spanish Bank East, Spanish Bank Extension, and Spanish Bank West. When the tide is out it looks like you could walk all the way across to the North Shore.

330 WRECK BEACH

AT: PACIFIC SPIRIT PARK
6344 University Blvd
University Endow-
ment Lands ⑫
wreckbeach.org

The city's only clothing-optional beach, Wreck Beach lies at the base of a cliff in Pacific Spirit Park near UBC. Access to the beach can be found in a couple of ways, most commonly via Trail 6, which includes a set of steep spiraling stairs. The clothing-optional section of the beach is marked and runs for nearly 7 km. As one of the most westerly spots in the city, the beach boasts impressive sunsets.

5 welcoming
LGBTQ+ SPOTS

331 MARY'S ON DAVIE

1202 Davie St
West End ③
+1 604 687 1293
marysondavie.com

Located in the heart of Davie Village, Mary's on Davie is the upscale diner you've been dreaming of. The restaurant is fun, with a bold interior of pastel pink, turquoise and palm print. Mary's is known for their perogies, boozy milkshakes, sass and community focused atmosphere.

332 THE JUNCTION PUBLIC HOUSE

1138 Davie St
West End ③
+1 604 669 2013

Open from 3 pm to 3 am daily, The Junction is a popular gay bar and night club in Davie Village. Whether it's queer improv, trivia night or drag bingo, there's something happening here almost every day of the week. Home to one of the best patios of Davie Street, a good pub menu, a packed dance floor and Top 40 hits.

333 LITTLE SISTERS BOOK & ART EMPORIUM

1238 Davie St
West End ③
+1 604 669 1753
littlesisters.ca

Opening its doors in 1983, Little Sisters has survived nearly four decades of challenges including changing governments and anti-gay harrassment. Referred to as Vancouver's 'grown-up general store', inside you'll find queer reads, coming out info, sexy literature, adult toys and the best greeting cards selection around.

334 QUEERS & BEERS
VARIOUS LOCATIONS
IN VANCOUVER
check Facebook

After growing tired of the 'white straight bearded masculinity' vibe that dominated the craft brewery scene, Ryn Broz decided to host the first Queers & Beers event. The nights are hosted seasonally and venues have included everything from local breweries and bars to converted warehouses. The atmosphere is relaxed and features plenty of local beer.

335 RAINBOW CROSSWALK
Intersection of
Bute St and Davie St
West End ③

Located at the intersection of Bute and Davie, this was Canada's first permanent rainbow crosswalk. The technicolour stripes were unveiled in July 2013 to kick off the city's Pride Week celebrations. The popular photo spot is situated next to Jim Deva Plaza, a memorial to Jim Deva, one the city's best known gay rights and anti-censorship activists.

335 RAINBOW CROSSWALK

ALLEY OOP

45 PLACES
FOR CULTURE

———————

5 exciting
FESTIVALS

336 **VANCOUVER CHERRY BLOSSOM FESTIVAL**
vcbf.ca

Running from the end of March to mid April, the Cherry Blossom Festival celebrates the arrival of spring in the city. Throughout the festival, there are events including Night Lights, a floral illumination display. Check out the Vancouver Cherry Blossom Festival website for the event guide and a live map of the best places to see the blossoms.

337 **DINE OUT VANCOUVER**
dineoutvancouver.com

Launched in 2003, Dine Out Vancouver is Canada's largest annual dining celebration. Beginning mid January and running 17 days, over 250 restaurants participate by offering unique three (or more)-course meals at 20, 30 or 40 dollar per person. The festival also includes food tours, cocktail masterclasses and global guest chef collaboration dinners.

338 CELEBRATION OF LIGHT

This is an annual international fireworks competition held over the course of three nights midsummer. Set to music and a theme, three fireworks companies representing different countries put on their best fireworks display with a winner chosen at the end of the festival. The pyrotechnics are lit from an offshore barge in English Bay.

336 VANCOUVER CHERRY BLOSSOM FESTIVAL

339 VANCOUVER MURAL FESTIVAL

vanmuralfest.ca

For 10 days every August, Create Vancouver Society hosts the annual Vancouver Mural Festival. On a mission to change the way the city sees art and highlight socio-cultural issues, the society invites artists to transform public spaces. The festival includes tours by donation, free live music and the Mount Pleasant Street Party. No worries if you miss the festival, there is an interactive map available online for self-guided tours.

340 PRIDE WEEK

vancouverpride.ca

Occurring in the first week of August, Pride Week in Vancouver is nothing short of a party! Events are hosted all week long in the build-up to the grand finale, the parade held on Sunday. Tens of thousands dressed in their best and brightest take to the streets to celebrate the LGBTQ+ community. The after-party at Sunset Beach should not be missed!

5 inspiring pieces of
PUBLIC ART

341 NOBODY LIKES ME
BY IHEART STENCILS
**Near the underpass
near Second Beach
Stanley Park** ④

Depicting an upset young boy with the Instagram notification bar showing zero comments, zero 'likes' and zero new followers above him, this piece of stenciled street art garnered international attention, including a nod from the graffiti king Banksy. The irony is not lost that photos of this has become a popular Instagram post.

342 THE BIRDS
BY MYFANWY MACLEOD
**Olympic Village Sq
Mount Pleasant** ⑧

Two larger than life sparrows call Olympic Village Square home. Standing at roughly five metres tall, the birds were installed just after the 2019 Winter Olympics. They are intended to remind Vancouverites and visitors of a few things: the city's sustainability, it's shipyard and immigration history and Alfred Hitchcock's horror film *The Birds*.

343 SHOULD I BE WORRIED?
BY JUSTIN LANGLOIS
Along the False Creek Seawall betw the Cambie Bridge and Habitat Island Mount Pleasant ⑧

Created by Vancouver's first ever Artist-in-Residence Justin Langlois, this neon sign sits atop a large wooden structure just east of the Cambie Street Bridge. The sign which reads 'SHOULD I BE WORRIED?' frames the incredibly expensive condos across the inlet and is a nod to the unaffordability of the Vancouver housing market. The artist worked with the Sustainability Group and it cost 65.000 dollar.

344 DIGITAL ORCA
BY DOUGLAS COUPLAND
AT: Vancouver Convention Centre West Building 1055 Canada Place Coal Harbour ③

Douglas Coupland's first piece of public art in Vancouver, the sculpture depicts a pixelated 25-foot-tall (7,6 metre) leaping killer whale. Made from steel armature with aluminium cladding, black and white cubes make up the whale's body. It's meant to draw attention to the importance of technology and nature to the city and consider the past, present and future of the site.

345 A-MAZE-ING LAUGHTER
BY YUE MINJUN
Morton Park West End ③

Either you love them or hate them, either way there's no denying these 14 bronze statues have become a landmark of the city. Created by artist Yue Minjun, they portray the artist's own image 'in a state of hysterical laughter'. The inscription at the base of the installation reads: "May this sculpture inspire laughter playfulness and joy in all who experience it."

344 DIGITAL ORCA

347 STANLEY PARK TOTEM POLES

The 5 best places to
EXPERIENCE FIRST NATIONS CULTURE

---

346 MUSEUM OF ANTHROPOLOGY
AT: UNIVERSITY OF BRITISH COLUMBIA
6393 NW Marine Dr University Endowment Lands ⑫
+1 604 827 5932
moa.ubc.ca

Founded in 1949 and located on the UBC campus, the museum has one of the world's most renowned collections of Northwest Coast First Nations arts and artifacts. The beautiful building, designed by Vancouver architect Arthur Erickson, houses close to 50.000 ethnographic objects and 535.000 archaeological objects. Don't miss acclaimed Haida artist Bill Reid's famous cedar statue *The Raven and the First Men*.

347 STANLEY PARK TOTEM POLES
Brockton Point Stanley Park ④
vancouver.ca

The nine totem poles located at Brockton Point in Stanley Park are British Columbia's most visited attraction. The collection started in the 1920s when the Park Board bought four totems from Alert Bay on Vancouver Island. The collection has since grown to nine with the most recent joining the group in 2009 carved by Robert Yelton of the Squamish Nation.

348 SALMON N' BANNOCK BISTRO

1128 W Broadway, #7
Fairview ⑦
+1 604 568 8971
salmonandbannock.net

The city's only First Nations restaurant, Salmon n' Bannock specializes in wild fish, free range game meat and bannock, a much loved First Nations flatbread. The team at the restaurant, many of whom are First Nations themselves, work to highlight indigenous cuisine of the Northwest Coast through the use of traditional ingredients. The bistro is casual and small, creating a warm and inviting gathering place.

349 BILL REID GALLERY OF NORTHWEST COAST ART

639 Hornby St
Downtown ②
+1 604 682 3455
billreidgallery.ca

Opened in 2008, this is Canada's only public gallery dedicated to contemporary indigenous art of the Northwest Coast. Named after Bill Reid, a master goldsmith, carver, sculptor, writer, broadcaster and spokesperson, the gallery is home to the Simon Fraser University Bill Reid Collection, as well as a number of other exhibits. Highlights of the gallery include Reid's statue *Mythic Messengers* and a totem pole by James Hart.

350 SKWACHÀYS LODGE AND URBAN ABORIGINAL FAIR TRADE GALLERY

29 W Pender St
Chinatown ②
+1 888 998 0797
skwachays.com

Created by the Vancouver Native Housing Society, the Skwachàys (pronounced *skwatch-eyes*) Lodge and Residence is a social enterprise. In the building there is a fair trade indigenous art gallery and boutique hotel, which support the indigenous artists in residence. The 18-unit hotel was recently refreshed, the gallery showcases indigenous work and there is a rooftop sweat lodge and smudge room.

5 *places to*
WATCH A GREAT SHOW

---

351 **COMMODORE BALLROOM**
868 Granville St
Downtown ②
+1 604 739 4550
commodore ballroom.com

Built in the late 1920s in the art deco style, the Commodore is known for being a fun and intimate venue. Inside you'll find multiple bars and booths and tables surrounding its famous sprung dance floor. Lined with horsehair, the floor absorbs impact from the dancing and jumping of concert goers.

352 **ORPHEUM**
601 Smithe St
Downtown ②
+1 604 665 3035
vancouvercivic theatres.com

Officially opened in 1927, the Orpheum was designed by architect Marcus Priteca. The antique interior features sweeping staircases, rich finishings and a domed roof auditorium capped off with a ceiling mural and crystal chandelier. The Orpheum is home to the Vancouver Symphony Orchestra, Western Canada's largest performing arts group.

353 MALKIN BOWL

610 Pipeline Road
Stanley Park ④
+1 855 985 5000
malkinbowl.com

Officially named The Marion Malkin Memorial Bowl, the Malkin Bowl is a 2000-seat outdoor theatre in Stanley Park. Built in 1934, it's a 2/3-size replica of the Hollywood Bowl in Los Angeles. Shows and productions run here from mid spring to mid fall and include the 'Theatre Under The Stars' Broadway musical series.

354 RICKSHAW THEATRE

254 E Hastings St
Chinatown ⑤
+1 604 681 8915
rickshawtheatre.com

Built in 1971 by the Shaw Brothers, Hong Kong film production moguls, the theatre was used as their west coast operations and distribution hub. In the mid-eighties, as interest in Kung-Fu movies faded, the theatre closed its doors until 2009, when it was repurposed into the outstanding music venue it is today.

355 THE VOGUE THEATRE

918 Granville St
Downtown ②
+1 604 688 1975
voguetheatre.com

Originally a movie house, The Vogue Theatre opened in 1941. Built in the art deco style, the theatre is located on 'Theatre Row' in the heart of the Entertainment District. In 1990 it was named a National Historic Site of Canada and is now an intimate performing arts venue with a capacity of just 1200 people.

5 great places for
LIVE MUSIC

---

356 **REVEL ROOM SUPPER CLUB**

238 Abbott St
Gastown ①
+1 604 687 4088
revelroom.ca

Revel Room brings a little bit of southern hospitality and charm to Gastown. They specialize in bourbon drinks but have all their bases covered. The real Revel standout is the local musicians making up the live entertainment. Phat Tuesdays, Rockabilly Wednesdays, Duelling Piano Thursdays… there is not a bad night of the week here.

357 **THE LOBBY LOUNGE AND RAWBAR**

1038 Canada Place Way
Coal Harbour ③
+1 604 695 5300
lobbyloungerawbar.com

The Lobby Lounge and RawBar at the Fairmont Pacific Rim is equal parts sophisticated and comfortable. Every night they host emerging artists, many of which play on their 225.000 dollar Fazioli piano. The cocktails are original and delightful and the food selection thoughtful, just like everything the Pacific Rim does.

358 GUILT & COMPANY

1 Alexander St,
Underground
Gastown ①
+1 604 288 1704
guiltandcompany.com

Take the stairs to the left of The Local in Gastown and step into Guilt & Company. Inside you'll find a dimly lit bar, tables and a small stage. This is Vancouver's 'biggest little stage' with performances every night. The bar menu has plenty to choose from, including 12 signature cocktails. We recommend the Baudelaire.

359 THE BILTMORE CABARET

2755 Prince Edward St
Mount Pleasant ⑧
+1 604 676 0541
biltmorecabaret.com

The Biltmore has been a fixture of the hip-hood of South Main for over 50 years. Throughout the week the venue hosts local and touring acts, comedy and trivia nights and just good old-fashioned themed music nights. The interior is dark with red velvet booths lining the walls. P.S. Birthdays here involve a lot of champagne!

360 THE BLARNEY STONE

216 Carrall St
Gastown ①
+1 604 687 4322
blarneystone.ca

Established in 1972, this is the longest-running Irish pub in the city and the closest thing to a Temple Bar experience you'll find in Vancouver. A relaxed Irish pub by day, things really kick off at night when the live Irish entertainment and atmosphere comes out in full force. The bar is multi-level, has plenty of tables and a dance floor.

5 top
ART GALLERIES

361 **THE VANCOUVER ART GALLERY**
750 Hornby St
Downtown ②
+1 604 662 4700
vanartgallery.bc.ca

Founded in 1931, the permanent collection of the gallery consists of 11.000 artworks including over 200 works by Emily Carr, The Group of Seven, Jeff Wall, Harry Callahan and Marc Chagall. The gallery hosts regular touring exhibits and lectures, it is home to a gift shop and a cute cafe. On Tuesday evenings from 5 to 9 pm admission is by donation.

362 **RENNIE MUSEUM**
AT: THE WING SANG BUILDING
51 E Pender St
Downtown ②
+1 604 682 2088
renniemuseum.org

Hidden behind the unassuming doors of the Rennie Museum is one of Canada's largest collections of contemporary art. Opened in 2009, the collection focuses on topics that surround identity, social commentary, injustice and appropriation. Entrance is free but the museum is only open to the public on Saturdays by appointment. Be sure to book ahead!

363 THE POLYGON GALLERY

101 Carrie Cates Court
North Vancouver ⑩
+1 604 986 1351
thepolygon.ca

Known previously as the Presentation House Gallery, this North Van gallery is the largest non-profit photographic gallery in Western Canada. Operating since 1981, The Polygon focuses on – but is not limited to – contemporary photography with an emphasis on Canadian work. The gallery itself is a modern and bright 25.000-square-feet (2322-square-metre) building with stunning water views.

364 MONTE CLARK GALLERY AND EQUINOX GALLERY

525 Great Northern Way, #105 + #110
Strathcona ⑤
+1 604 730 5000 (MC)
+1 604 736 2405 (EQ)
monteclarkgallery.com
equinoxgallery.com

Next door neighbours to each other, the Monte Clark Gallery and Equinox Gallery are both contemporary galleries exhibiting local, national and select international up-and-coming and established artists. The galleries have similar industrial-chic interiors and are tucked behind the prestigious Emily Carr University of Art + Design's new campus.

365 CATRIONA JEFFRIES

950 E Cordova St
Downtown Eastside ⑤
+1 604 736 1554
catrionajeffries.com

Established in 1994, this is one of the few Vancouver galleries to have an international reputation. The contemporary gallery focuses on post-conceptual art and shows work from well-known local artists such as Ian Wallace and Brian Jungen. Everything about the gallery has been deeply considered, including the 'urban void' gravel garden. Each crunchy footstep transitions you from the outside to the inside.

The 5 most
GRAM-ABLE STREET MURALS

---

366 NO RAIN NO FLOWERS
BY THRIVE ART STUDIO
**Betw 7th and 8th
Avenue near Main St
Mount Pleasant** ⑧

As much as Vancouverites know the rain keeps the city beautiful, sometimes we forget. The soft pink and navy *No Rain No Flowers* mural, however, is a good reminder. To quote the artists: "Just like all great things in life you don't get the reward without the work. You don't get the flowers without the rain."

367 VANCOUVER STUDIO (AFTER MATISSE)
BY ANDY DIXON
**4th Avenue betw
Quebec and Main
Mount Pleasant** ⑧

North Van native Andy Dixon has been making waves in the art world with his mesmerizing and colourful paintings. His work showcases around the world and sells for tens-of-thousands of dollars. His contribution to the 2017 Mural Fest allows passersby a glimpse into his nearby Vancouver studio. The paintings propped up within the mural are full-scale replicas of paintings he has completed.

368 ALLEY OOP

BY HCMA IN PARTNERSHIP
WITH CITY OF VANCOUVER
AND THE DOWNTOWN
VANCOUVER BUSINESS
IMPROVEMENT
ASSOCIATION
688 W Hastings St
Downtown ②

More than just a mural, Alley Oop is meant to be an urban space for people to come play! Located in an alley south of Hastings between streets Granville and Seymour, the mural was completed in 2016 and features a small basketball court and hopscotch. It's rare to come to the pastel thoroughfare without seeing a photoshoot of some type going down.

369 RIDE WILD

BY CARSON TING
143 E 3rd Avenue
Mount Pleasant ⑧

This 98-foot by 16-foot-tall (30 by 5 metre) mural took seven days to complete. The painting is meant to be a fun portrayal of the mindset of a Vancouver commuter, basically to cycle or not to cycle. Designed as an augmented reality piece, download the Generate app and watch the mural come to life!

370 #KITSWINGS

BY SANDY PELL
Northwest corner
of Burrard St and
W 4th Avenue
Kitsilano ⑦

Inspired by the bald eagles living nearby, artist Sandy Pell created the 40-foot by 25-foot (12 by 7,5 metre) winged wall mural with her husband Steve. The mandala-like outline behind the wings is based on the stunning Kitsilano sunsets and sunrises, painted in gold metallic paint "to almost grab the sun as it shines onto the wall". Stand in front, snap a pic and look like an angel.

5 VANCOUVER-BASED ARTISTS

to get to know

---

371 EMILY CARR
1871-1945

Born in 1871, Emily Carr is considered a Canadian icon. Inspired by the Pacific Northwest Coast, her paintings captured aboriginal themes and vivid landscapes. Carr was one of the first Canadians to use a modernist and post-impressionist style. Emily Carr University of Art + Design is one of the most prestigious art schools in the country.

372 DOUGLAS COUPLAND
1961

Known predominantly as a writer, Coupland has published countless written works including international best-seller *Generation X: Tales for an Accelerated Culture*. His visual artwork often has themes of pop culture, 20th-century pop art and military imagery having grown up in a military family. For his contributions he was awarded the Order of Canada in 2013.

373 **ANDY DIXON**
1979

A North Van native, prior to taking up painting full-time Dixon was a punk rocker. The first thing you'll notice when you look at one of his pieces is the colours, he uses pastels dominated by bright reds, yellows and teals. Much of his work is centered around luxury goods and the psychology of value.

374 **BRIAN JUNGEN**
1970

Jungen creates contemporary pieces known for connecting his First Nations ancestry, Western art history and the economy. Practising found object art, he reworks the objects to fully conceal them in a piece. For his *Prototypes of New Understanding* series, he built aboriginal masks from parts of Nike Air Jordan shoes.

375 **COLLEEN HESLIN**
1976

Currently represented by the Monte Clarke Gallery, Heslin is known for her mixed medium work using textiles and quilting to create abstract pieces which she calls paintings. Her textile paintings use previously owned, hand-dyed fabrics which are then sewn and stretched.

The 5 best
CINEMAS

—————

376 **RIO THEATRE**
1660 E Broadway
Commercial Drive ⑥
+1 604 879 3456
riotheatre.ca

Built in 1938, the Rio is located on the bustling corner of Broadway and Commercial. An independent art house, the fully restored venue hosts a wide variety of entertainment including live shows, late-night movie screenings and live-streamed events like the Oscars and Barack Obama's 2008 inauguration.

377 **TWILIGHT DRIVE-IN**
260th St & Fraser
Highway
Langley ⑫
+1 604 856 5063
twilightdrivein.net

Opened in 2005, the Twilight Drive-In is the only drive-in theatre in Metro Vancouver. Open mid-February to November, admission to the theatre includes not just one but all the movies playing that night. The movie audio is broadcasted over FM radio into your vehicle and retro concession ads play before each show.

378 **DUNBAR THEATRE**
4555 Dunbar St
Dunbar ⑫
+1 604 222 2991

Dunbar Theatre has the touch of charm that all independent theatres should have. Boasting large, comfy seats, the cinema is outside of the busy city-centre and is rarely crowded. Most notably, they have the best buttered popcorn in the city.

379 FIFTH AVENUE CINEPLEX

2110 Burrard St
Fairview ⑦
+1 604 734 7469
cineplex.com

An adults-only theatre, this modern cinema includes a full bar alongside its concession stand. The multi-screen theatre shows mainstream flicks and indie favourites. The screens are large and so are the reclining seats. Grab a beer or glass of wine to pair with your popcorn and settle into the show.

380 THE CINEMATHEQUE

1131 Howe St
Yaletown ②
+1 604 688 8202
thecinematheque.ca

This small, 192-seat neighbourhood theatre located on the edges of Yaletown focuses on the 'art and history of Canadian and international cinema'. Run by a local film society, it features films outside of mainstream Hollywood, curating them similar to that of an art museum. Have no fear though, there is still a concession to grab snacks before the show.

376 RIO THEATRE

SCIENCE WORLD AT TELUS WORLD OF SCIENCE

15 THINGS TO DO WITH CHILDREN

5 cute
SHOPS FOR KIDS

---

381 KIDSBOOKS

2557 W Broadway
Kitsilano ⑦
+1 604 738 5335
kidsbooks.ca

The experts in town in children's books, the helpful staff at Kidsbooks in Kitsilano are always ready with a recommendation. Interactive readings are held regularly, as well as local and touring authors. Outside of books, the friendly shop carries a selection of great toys and stuffed animals.

382 GRANVILLE ISLAND KIDS MARKET

1496 Cartwright St
Granville Island ⑤
+1 604 689 8447
kidsmarket.ca

With two floors packed with toys, crafts, magic, games and candy, this warehouse-style market is a perfect place to let the kids run wild. Everything about the market is 'kid-centric', including the hair salon and kids-sized doors. The Adventure Zone, a multi-level play area, is a good spot to let the kids burn off some energy.

383 BEANSPROUTS

4305 Main St
Riley Park ⑨
+1 604 871 9782
beansprouts.ca

You never know what treasures you'll find at this cheerful children's boutique. With a play area for kids, this partly consignment shop is perfect for the environment- and price-conscious shopper. All of the 'pre-loved' pieces are carefully selected and they offer sizes from newborn to ten years old.

384 DILLY DALLY

1161 Commercial Dr
Commercial Drive ⑥
+1 604 252 9727
dillydallykids.ca

The folks at Dilly Dally have done the research and know their toys. With a focus on 'inspiring play', owners Claire and Tyler truly believe toys are important tools for growing kids. The bright and fun shop carries high-quality educational toys that inspire creativity and imagination.

385 HIP BABY

2110 W 4th Avenue
Kitsilano ⑦
+1 604 736 8020
hipbaby.com

A go-to shop for all things baby, toddlers and kids, this Kitsilano boutique has earned a reputation for its great customer service and diverse thoughtful products. Re-opened in 2009, shoppers can find a wide selection of organic and modern kids goods including toys, cloth diapers, baby carriers and apparel, many of which are local or Canadian made.

384 DILLY DALLY

5 ADVENTUROUS ACTIVITIES *to do with kids*

386 PLAYLAND AT THE PNE

2901 E Hastings St
Hastings-Sunrise ⑩
+1 604 253 2311
pne.ca/playland

The oldest amusement park in Canada, visitors to Playland will find rides, games and tasty treats. Adrenaline junkies can't miss a ride on the Wooden Roller Coaster. Built in 1958 and reaching speeds of 45 mph (72 km), the coaster has been named the top wooden coaster in Canada and one of the best in the world.

387 STANLEY PARK TRAIN

690 Pipeline Road
Stanley Park ④
+1 604 257 8531

Popular with locals and tourists, the Stanley Park Train is a 2-kilometre, 15-minute ride through a section of the park's forest. The train is open all year but has different themes depending on the season, the most popular being the Ghost Train in fall and the Bright Nights during the holidays. The train is a good way to experience Stanley Park for those who are less mobile.

388 GRANVILLE ISLAND WATER PARK

1318 Cartwright St
Granville Island ⑦
+1 604 257 8195

Open weekends from May to June, and seven days a week from July to September, the water park is a favourite spot for city kids to cool down. With plenty of sprayers and fountains and a slippery slide, the park is completely free and has a grass area for families to relax.

389 MAPLEWOOD FARM

405 Seymour River Pl
North Vancouver ⑲
+1 604 929 5610
maplewoodfarm.bc.ca

Found 20 minutes from downtown in North Vancouver, Maplewood Farm is open rain or shine all year. Home to over 200 animals including birds, cows, goats, horses, pigs, rabbits, sheep and donkeys, the farm offers people of all ages to get up close with animals and learn about them. The pony rides are very popular and there is a picnic area for visitors.

390 GNARLY'S SNOW TUBING PARK

6000 Cypress Bowl Rd
North Vancouver ⑲
+1 604 926 5612
cypressmountain.com/
snowtubing

Opening with the ski season, Gnarly's Tube Park is a great way to get outside and nature in the winter. With six runs 100 metres in length, shoot down the hill and then grab the tube tow to bring you back to the top and do it all over again! For those 6 and under, there is a sliding area close by. Don't forget to pre-book!

The 5 best spots
TO LEARN SOMETHING

391 SCIENCE WORLD AT TELUS WORLD OF SCIENCE

1455 Quebec St
Downtown ②
+1 604 443 7440
scienceworld.ca

The geometric dome of Science World is an iconic building in the Vancouver skyline. Inside you'll find interactive science displays and films for learners of all ages. Look out for touring exhibits and don't miss catching a show in the OMNIMAX, with its wrap-around sound system and at 5 storeys high and 27 metres in diameter, it's the largest dome screen in the world.

392 H.R. MACMILLAN SPACE CENTRE

AT: VANIER PARK
1100 Chestnut St
Kitsilano ⑦
+1 604 738 7827
spacecentre.ca

Located 15 minutes from downtown in Kitsilano's Vanier Park, the HR MacMillan Space Centre is B.C.'s top space attraction. With a mission to 'educate and inspire and evoke wonder', the space centre has been increasing space literacy since 1968. Be sure to catch a show at the Planetarium Star Theatre! The reclined seats and concave ceiling screen makes for an out-of-this-world experience.

393 VANCOUVER AQUARIUM
AT: STANLEY PARK
845 Avison Way
Stanley Park ④
+1 604 659 3474
vanaqua.org

Officially Canada's first public aquarium, Vancouver Aquarium is a world leader in marine conservation and research. Home to over 50.000 animals and 30 unique exhibits, opportunities to learn something at the aquarium are endless. Check the schedule to see what events and shows are on for the day. You can get up close and personal with some creatures by booking an Encounter experience.

394 GROUSE MOUNTAIN GRIZZLY BEAR HABITAT
6400 Nancy Greene Way
North Vancouver ⑲
+1 604 980 9311
grousemountain.com/wildlife-refuge

Home to two orphaned grizzly bears, Grinder and Coola moved into their five-acre refuge on Grouse Mountain in 2001. The bears have since called the mountain home and can be regularly be seen hanging out in their pond or play fighting. Join a Ranger Talk to learn more about the animals in the Wildlife Refuge or sign up to have Breakfast with the Bears!

395 BURNABY VILLAGE MUSEUM
6501 Deer Lake Ave
Burnaby ⑫
+1 604 297 4565
burnabyvillage museum.ca

A visit to Burnaby Village Museum is the closest thing you'll get to visit the 1920's. Take a walk through the fictional town and chat with the townsfolk who will welcome you into their homes and shops. The pièce de résistance is the 1912 carousel. The museum is a great spot to take the kids on a rainy day.

FREE SPIRIT SPHERES

20 PLACES
TO SLEEP

The 5 most
HIGH-END HOTELS

396 FAIRMONT PACIFIC RIM

1038 Canada Place
Coal Harbour ③
+1 604 695 5300
fairmont.com/
pacific-rim-vancouver

The flagship location of the Fairmont Hotel Group, the Pac Rim offers stunning five-star sleeps and amenities, and is home to the most expensive hotel room in the city. For 15.000 dollar a night you can stay in the two-storey 2250-square-foot (209-square-metre) Chairman's Suite, which includes an outdoor fireplace, a private elevator, a hand carved tub and a reflection pool.

397 ROSEWOOD HOTEL GEORGIA

801 W Georgia St
Downtown ②
+1 604 682 5566
rosewoodhotels.com/
hotel-georgia-vancouver

First opening its doors in 1927, the Hotel Georgia recently underwent an extensive renovation. Still keeping its historic charm, the 156-room hotel is known for its superior service, art deco interior, stunning salt water lap pool and incredibly central location. It's home to arguably the city's best restaurant Hawksworth and the sleek Prohibition jazz bar.

398 SHANGRI-LA HOTEL

1128 W Georgia St
Coal Harbour ③
+1 604 689 1120
shangri-la.com/
vancouver

Built with the guidance of a feng shui master and blessed by monks, even the smallest of the 119 rooms are good size, have luxury finishings and feature beautiful art. At 62 storeys it is the tallest building in Vancouver and the floor-to-ceiling windows in each room take full advantage of the city skyline views.

399 THE DOUGLAS, AUTOGRAPH COLLECTION

45 Smithe St
Downtown ②
+1 604 676 0889
parqvancouver.com/
hotels/the-douglas

Overlooking False Creek, the DOUGLAS is inspired by Vancouver's unique nature and cosmopolitan combo. One of two hotels connected to Parq Vancouver, the city's premier entertainment destination, the interior features a bold urban aesthetic. Check out the D/6 Bar and Lounge patio, play a little at Parq and experience the hotel's exceptional service.

400 WEDGEWOOD HOTEL + SPA

845 Hornby St
Downtown ②
+1 604 689 7777
wedgewoodhotel.com

Across the street from the Vancouver Art Gallery, this family-owned hotel is old-school luxury. Guests here are greeted by a top-hatted doorman and a rich interior of classic wood panelling, plush carpet and hunting prints. Despite being in the centre of the city, it has a high-end countryside estate atmosphere paired with tip-top service.

5 wonderful
BOUTIQUE SLEEPS

401 THE BURRARD

1100 Burrard St
Downtown ②
+1 604 681 2331
theburrard.com

Formerly a motor hotel from 1956, this hotel is situated downtown, between trendy Yaletown and the beachy-fun West End. The hotel combines mid-century modern with contemporary designs and a touch of 1950s groove. The hotel wraps around a lush central courtyard, perfect for chilling out after a day of sightseeing.

402 LODEN

1177 Melville St
Coal Harbour ③
+1 604 669 5060
theloden.com

Conveniently located in Coal Harbour, this luxury boutique hotel is ultra cool. The decor is modern and sleek, with punchy pops of colour. They are known for their eye for detail and sincere staff, as well as the floor-to-ceiling windows found in the beautiful rooms.

403 HOTEL BLU

177 Robson St
Downtown ②
+1 604 620 6200
hotelbluvancouver.com

This upscale hotel's motto is 'luxury and technology meet sustainability'. This high tech spot is not without its comforts however, with chic rooms and facilities, they offer complimentary yoga and a tablet loaded with entertainment. Stay after stay, BLU proves that going green can still look and feel good.

404 OPUS HOTEL

322 Davie St
Yaletown ②
+1 866 642 6787
vancouver.opushotel.com

Perhaps the most stylish sleep in the city, the OPUS Hotel is consistently named one of the best hotels in Canada. The designer rooms have contemporary-chic interiors with bold colours, mod furnishings and feng-shui bed placements. On site you'll also find the sleek OPUS bar and La Pentola restaurant serving classic Italian.

405 THE LISTEL HOTEL

1300 Robson St
West End ③
+1 604 684 8461
thelistelhotel.com

If you ever wanted to stay in an art gallery, this is as close as you might get. Named the city's 'most artful hotel', each and every room in The Listel Hotel is designed as an individual gallery featuring limited edition prints and original artwork. Additionally, the hotel is committed to the environment and has been 100% waste-free since 2011.

401 THE BURRARD

The 5 best
CAMPGROUNDS

406 ALICE LAKE PROVINCIAL PARK

Along the BC-99
Squamish ⑪
+1 604 986 9371
discovercamping.ca

This park is a favourite for its mountain views, dense forests and four freshwater lakes, Edith, Stump, Fawn and Alice. In addition to the hiking and mountain biking trails close by there is swimming, picnicking, fishing, canoeing and stand-up paddleboarding. Facilities include two shower and washroom buildings, an amphitheatre, playground and the Beachside Café.

407 GOLDEN EARS PROVINCIAL PARK

24480 Fern Crescent
Maple Ridge ⑫
discovercamping.ca

Just an hour outside of the city, Golden Ears Provincial Park is one of the largest parks in the province and is prized for its wide variety of activities available including swimming, windsurfing, water-skiing, canoeing, boating and fishing. There are three campgrounds to choose from, with Gold Creek being our favourite. Alouette Lake is crystal clear and the mountains surrounding are stunning.

408 CHILLIWACK LAKE PROVINCIAL PARK

Trans Canada Trail
Rosedale
discovercamping.ca

If it weren't for the evergreen trees and surrounding mountains, the soft white sand and crystal clear water of Chilliwack Lake could double as somewhere in the Bahamas. Located a 150 kilometres east of Vancouver, the campground has over 40 kilometres of trails, plenty of on-water activities and nearly 150 frontcountry campsites.

409 FORT CAMPING

9451 Glover Road
Fort Langley ⑬
+1 604 888 3678
fortcamping.com

Located on the Fraser River, this campground puts you just across the river from the darling historic Fort Langley. A former fur trade post for the Hudson's Bay Company, in the village you'll find an endless selection of cute shops, cafes and restaurants. Stop at Wendel's Bookstore & Café and take a stroll along the river.

410 MTN FUN BASECAMP

1796 Depot Road
Squamish ⑪
+1 604 390 4200
mtnfunbasecamp.com

Even though you'll be only minutes away from shops and restaurants, you'll still feel completely surrounded by nature here. The team here make camping easy and fun, with tent sites, RV hook-ups and clean comfortable hotel suites up for grabs. Additionally, there are rentals available, a small camp store with essentials, BBQ's, fire pits and Wi-Fi.

5 beautiful **GLAMPING LOCATIONS**

411 **WOODS ON PENDER**

4709 Canal Road
Pender Island ⑫
+1 250 629 3353
woodsonpender.com

This modern camping experience located on Pender Island offers four unique accommodation styles: Airstreams, Shasta Airflyte, Rustic Cabins, and the WOODS Motel. With all the comforts of home inside and the beauty of the West Coast on the outside, the tranquil facility also includes Coffee + Kitchen, WOODS Massage and all the activities a Gulf Island has to offer.

412 **FREE SPIRIT SPHERES**

420 Horne Lake Rd
Vancouver Island
+1 250 757 9445
freespiritspheres.com

Look up, look waaaay up! These one-of-a-kind spherical treehouses are the perfect mix of getting back to nature and glamping. The spheres are made in the practice of Biomimicry – a sustainable solution that emulates nature. Roughly 3 metres in diameter, the spheres are made to sleep two people and is tethered to three different trees.

413 **WILD HAVENS**

+1 778 806 5082
wildhavens.ca

Wild Havens is a pop-up mobile business that specializes in creating glamping experiences for customers – you choose your own location and Wild Havens will set everything up for you before you arrive! You can choose tents that sleep up to 6 people, so grab a group of friends and be at one with nature!

414 **WILDPOD GLAMPING**

174 West St
Tofino
+1 250 725 2020
wildpod.ca

Comprised of six geodesic domes, WILDPOD is luxury waterfront glamping at its finest. The resort is perched on the water's edge just outside of downtown Tofino with everything you could possibly need within walking distance. Each pod offers tasteful but lush interiors as well as amazing water views, perfect for watching the wildlife and the sunset.

415 **BODEGA COVE**

18680 Porlier Pass Rd
Galiano Island
+1 877 604 2677
bodegaridge.com

Newly restored, Bodega Cove features five beautiful Panabode timber cabins, each cozy but tastefully furnished. Nestled on the coast of Galiano Island, it has views of the broken islands, the mountains of Vancouver Island and is surrounded by fir trees. If you make it to Bodega Cove, make sure to book a reservation at Pilgrimme, recently named one of the best new restaurants in Canada.

STAWAMUS CHIEF

50 WEEKEND ACTIVITIES

---

5 unforgettable
DAY HIKES

416 QUARRY ROCK

2505 Panorama Dr
North Vancouver ⑩

Want to do a hike but don't have all day? Quarry Rock in North Vancouver takes a quick 45 minutes to get to the rocky outcrop viewpoint which looks down upon the community of Deep Cove and the Indian Arm inlet. After the hike, head on over to Honey Doughnuts for a well-deserved treat.

417 STAWAMUS CHIEF

BC-99,
Britannia Beach,
BC V0N 1J0
Squamish ⑪

Commonly known as 'The Chief', this hike is a Vancouver classic. With its three peaks and mountain's famous silhouette, the trail has some challenging but fun sections, with ladders and chains to help you along the way. The view from the top looks down on to the city of Squamish and the beautiful Howe Sound.

420 **ELFIN LAKES**

418 GARIBALDI LAKE
AT: GARIBALDI
PROVINCIAL PARK
Daisy Lake Road
Whistler ⑪

With turquoise-coloured water nestled between alpine mountains and a breathtaking glacier as the backdrop, the Garibaldi Lake hike is nothing short of breathtaking. Stop at the lake for a refreshing swim and a bite to eat or continue on to Panorama Ridge to get a view from above. Warning – the distance and elevation gain makes for a very long day.

419 DOG MOUNTAIN
1700 Mt Seymour Rd
North Vancouver ⑲

Starting from the top of Mount Seymour, on a clear day this short hike offers breathtaking views of the city. The return trip is roughly 5 kilometres with little elevation gain making it possible to complete the trail and still enjoy the view all under two hours. However, it's worth mentioning some sections of the path require careful stepping due to slippery tree roots.

420 ELFIN LAKES
AT: GARIBALDI
PROVINCIAL PARK
Diamond Head Trail
Parking Lot
Whistler ⑪

Located in Garibaldi Provincial Park, Elfin Lakes are two alpine lakes surrounded by impressive mountain views. One lake is for swimming, the other for drinking water. With an elevation gain of 600 metres over 22 kilometres, while the trail is long, it is one of the easier hikes in the park. Popular with hikers, bikers and skiers, there are 35 tent pads and a large backcountry hut available for permit holders use.

5 breweries to visit on your
MOUNT PLEASANT BREWERY CREEK CRAWL

421 33 ACRES BREWING COMPANY

15 W 8th Avenue
Mount Pleasant ⑧
+1 604 620 4589
33acresbrewing.com

Inspired by the binding elements of life, this Mount Pleasant brewery is a staple of the Vancouver beer scene. The tasting room is bright with minimal but stylish decor. If you have adventurous taste buds check out 33 Brew Exp next door where the team is constantly experimenting with new flavours and brew techniques. Start your tour here to have some brunch with your beer.

422 R&B ALE & PIZZA HOUSE

1-54 E 4th Avenue
Mount Pleasant ⑧
+1 604 336 0275
randbbrewing.com

Is there a better pair than pizza and beer? One of Vancouver's original microbreweries, R&B opened its doors in 1997 and has been producing handcrafted ales and lagers ever since. Their Vancouver Special IPA was named the best IPA in B.C. and pairs perfectly with any of their artisanal pizzas.

421 **33 ACRES BREWING COMPANY**

423 ELECTRIC BICYCLE BREWING

20 E 4th Avenue
Mount Pleasant ⑧
+1 604 709 9939
*electricbicyle
brewing.com*

A brewery experience like no other! Inspired by their favourite record shops and art spaces, the team at Electric Bicycle have created an electric space through the loud decor and ever changing art. All of that paired with their tasty tap list and unreal grilled cheese sandwiches makes for a sensational experience and a memorable stop on your brewery crawl.

424 MAIN ST BREWING

261 E 7th Avenue
Mount Pleasant ⑧
+1 604 336 7711
mainstreetbeer.ca

Tucked inside a historic brewery building that dates back to 1913, the space which is now home to Main St Brewing once belonged to the powerhouse that was Vancouver Breweries. The tasting room has an industrial feel with high ceilings and aged exposed brick, warmed up with long wooden high-tables and strings of lights. Their Main Street Pilsner is a tried and true favourite.

425 BRASSNECK BREWERY

2148 Main St
Mount Pleasant ⑧
+1 604 259 7686
brassneck.ca

Brassneck Brewery is the brainchild from two of Vancouver's biggest craft beer pioneers, Alibi Room owner Nigel Springthorpe and long time Steamworks Head Brewer Conrad Gmoser. The team here loves to experiment, just 3.5 years and they had already brewed over 120 different beers. The small tasting room is designed to make visitors feel a part of the process, with the brewhouse and cellar wrapping around it.

5 *fantastic*
WEEKEND ESCAPES

426 WHISTLER

Whistler ⑪

An under-two-hour drive from Vancouver, Whistler is a major destination for tourists and locals. Consistently voted one of the best ski resorts in the world, the mountain setting is breathtaking. Accommodation options include the finest 5-star hotels to tent campgrounds. Top activities including skiing, snowboarding, hiking, bungee jumping, lake swimming, shopping, dining, relaxing and partying – there really is something for everyone.

427 SEATTLE (USA)

Drive two and a half hours south and you'll find yourself in Seattle. As a fellow Pacific Northwest town, The Emerald City shares many similarities with Vancouver including, a lot of rain. Home of Starbucks, Boeing, Microsoft, Amazon and Nirvana, Seattlelites are known for their love of music, sports teams, great coffee and food. Check out the famous Pike Place Market but don't miss some of the cool surrounding neighbourhoods, like Ballard and Capitol Hill.

428 OKANAGAN

Also known as the Okanagan Valley, the region covers of 71.000 km² and includes over 90 communities, with the primary city being Kelowna. The area is most prominently known for being the wine region of B.C., with 40 wineries within a 20-minute drive from Kelowna alone. Additionally, the Valley is popular in the summer for its warmer weather, lakes and camping. In the winter people make their way to one of the many ski resorts.

429 VICTORIA

Vancouver Island
South of Vancouver ⑫

The capital city of British Columbia, Victoria is a 90-minute ferry ride across the Strait of Georgia to Vancouver Island. The downtown has a charming British feel to it, influenced by the architecture of the Parliament Buildings, Empress Hotel, harbour and pubs and shops that line the streets. Within the city you'll find museums, castles, gardens galore and plenty of beaches to explore.

430 SALT SPRING ISLAND

South of Vancouver ⑫

A wonderful option for those looking for a quiet escape, the beautiful Salt Spring Island is one of 200 Gulf Islands located between the mainland and Vancouver Island. As with most of the Gulf Islands, Salt Spring is known for its laidback, organic vibe but as the most populous island it has the widest variety of accommodation and activity options.

5 fun **ADVENTUROUS ACTIVITIES** *to try*

431 **WHITE WATER RAFTING**

Some of the best river rafting in North America can be found within a short distance of the city. The Thompson, the Nahatlatch, the Squamish, the Elaho and the Chilliwack Rivers all have heart pumping rapids and guide companies close by to take you safely through them.

432 **ZIPLINING**

Ziplining is a great way to see the beauty of our temperate rainforests from a fun and fast perspective. Zip through the dense forests and over running rivers and throughout the year locally on Grouse Mountain or if you make it up to Whistler, check out Ziptrek Ecotours' 'The Sasquatch', it's the longest zipline in North America at two kilometres long.

433 BUNGEE JUMPING

Cal-Cheak Forest
Service Road
Whistler ⑪
+1 604 938 9333
whistlerbungee.com

For those looking to really get their pulse up look no further than Whistler Bungee. Located close to the Village, you'll take the leap 50 metres above the glacial-fed Cheakamus River surrounded by an old-growth forest and basalt column cliffs. Their team of jump masters and operators have a spotless safety record.

434 ROCK CLIMBING

Squamish and the Sea-to-Sky Corridor is world-famous for its climbing and bouldering. If you're new to the sport there are plenty of local guide companies to teach you the ropes, literally. Rock climbing season runs from late April to early October but there are a ton of indoor gyms all over the town for bad weather days.

435 KITESURFING

Growing in popularity year after year, there are top-quality kitesurfing locations sprinkled all over the Lower Mainland, including Ambleside Beach, Crescent Beach, Porteau Cove and The Spit Squamish, one of the world's best spots to take the kite and board out in North America.

The 5 best locations to
GET ON THE WATER

---

436 FALSE CREEK
AT: CREEKSIDE KAYAK
RENTAL
1495 Ontario St
Mount Pleasant ⑧
+1 604 616 7453
creeksidekayaks.ca

Being able to kayak and paddleboard in the heart of the city is one of the things that sets Vancouver apart from others. Get onboard in Olympic Village and start exploring False Creek and the harbour. Paddling under the Cambie Bridge while taking in views of the city and eventually Granville Island.

437 BUNTZEN LAKE
AT: ANMORE STORE &
RECREATION LTD
3275 Sunnyside Road
Anmore ⑩
+1 604 469 9928

Located just north of the community of Anmore, the lake is about a 45-minute drive from downtown. In addition to being jaw-droppingly gorgeous, it is an active hydroelectric reservoir and at one point was a main producer of electricity for the city. Hop in a kayak or canoe from the rental shop at the park's entrance and get exploring!

438 DEEP COVE

AT: DEEP COVE KAYAK
CENTRE
2156 Banbury Road
North Vancouver ⑩
+1 604 929 2268
deepcovekayaks.com

While not far out of the city, Deep Cove feels incredibly secluded. The local rental shop offers kayak, canoe and stand-up-paddleboards by the hour, as well as guided tours and lessons. Paddle up the Indian Arm fjord, the water is generally very smooth and is a great showcase of the Pacific Northwest coastline.

439 ROCKY POINT PARK

AT: ROCKY POINT KAYAK
2805 Esplanade Ave
Port Moody ⑩
+1 604 936 1112
rockypointkayak.com

Accessible by SkyTrain, Rocky Point Park is situated on the most eastern part of the Burrard Inlet. Kayak and canoe rentals are available in the park and the water is full of harbour seals. After your paddle, grab some ice cream at Rocky Point Ice Cream or if you'd rather a cold one, check out Brewers Row, a collection of craft breweries across the street.

440 PITT LAKE

AT: PITT LAKE CANOE
ADVENTURES
Pitt Meadows
+1 604 836 7117

About an hour west of Vancouver you'll find Pitt Lake, the second largest lake in the Lower Mainland. Popular with wildlife photographers, cyclists and walkers, the lake is surrounded by mountains and marshlands. Canoe rentals are available at the boat launch. Take them up the creek and complete the Widgeon Falls trail for a full day of the great outdoors.

The 5 best
YOGA CLASSES

**441 SEMPERVIVA YOGA –
SEA STUDIO**

1333 Johnston St,
#200
Granville Island ⑤
+1 604 739 2009
semperviva.com

Semperviva is dedicated to guiding powerful and authentic yoga experiences. They offer a wide variety of classes and host one of the most popular teacher training programs in the city. The Sea Studio on Granville Island is the location to check out. It has windows overlooking the water and a 180-degree view of downtown.

441 SEMPERVIVA YOGA – SEA STUDIO

442 MODO YOGA

2083 Alma St, #242
Kitsilano ⑦
+1 604 569 3650
vancouver.
modoyoga.com

This is the studio for you if you're looking for a gentle butt-kicking. Classes combine a series of postures to help you strengthen and stretch your body whilst in the heated studio. The studio focuses on the six Pillars: be healthy, be accessible, live green, support community, live to learn, and be peace.

443 ONE YOGA FOR THE PEOPLE

150 W Hastings St,
#201
Gastown ①
+1 604 710 7267
oneyogafor
thepeople.com

One Yoga for the People is known for their long and powerful vinyasa classes and strong, supportive community. The studio is bright and friendly and believes that no matter your age, ability, gender, race, religion or financial status, yoga is for you. They stand by this by offering by donation drop-in options.

444 DHARMA TEMPLE

3283 Main St
Riley Park ⑨
+1 604 559 8507
thedharmatemple.com

Dharma Yoga offers a more spiritual and traditional yoga experience. In addition to the challenging but accessible yoga classes, the studio has a variety of classes which include meditation, pilates, hatha, circus and master classes. A soulful place to be, you'll leave feeling refreshed and calm.

445 OUTDOOR YOGA
VARIOUS LOCATIONS

matcollective.com

Starting out as a recycling program to keep unwanted yoga mats from the landfill has grown into a Vancouver staple. Throughout the summer Mat Collective hosts free outdoor yoga classes at Kits Beach, Main Street, Downtown and Granville Island. Classes run rain or shine!

5 motivating places to
GET FIT

---

446 CLUB ROW
163 W Pender St
Downtown ②
+1 604 562 8754
clubrowfitness.com

Vancouver's first row studio, Club Row took all the best parts of a spin class and made it their own. The boutique fitness spot comes through with upbeat music, high intensity workouts, fun choreography and a strong community vibe. The row studio is industrial chic with a sprinkle of tropical.

447 TANTRA FITNESS
314 Water St
Gastown ①
+1 604 738 7653
tantrafitness.com

Pole dancing is a hard workout. Don't believe it? The team at Tantra will prove it to you. As the number one pole dancing studio in Vancouver, they have award-winning instructors, a beautiful facility and fun classes. They also teach a variety of dance classes and aerial arts.

448 TIGHT CLUB
261 Union St
Chinatown ⑤
+1 604 620 0209
tightclubathletics.com

The team at Tight Club believe exercise doesn't have to define you, it's there to enhance you. Offering everything from pilates to plyometrics and mobility training to HIIT, each workout is fresh and fun. A fitness place for all, this is a welcoming community of people who just like to get their sweat on.

449 ALL-CITY ATHLETICS

130 W Hastings St
Gastown ①
+1 604 559 7413
allcityathletics.ca

Located in Gastown, this underground boxing studio's motto is 'Work Hard. Stay Humble'. Staying true to proper boxing technique, the fitness and training classes are the good kind of grind, working both your body and your brain. The instructors helping you build your skills are experienced and motivating, and the gym is edgy-cool.

450 EASTWOOD CYCLE

154 W Hastings St
Gastown ①
+1 604 899 3278
eastwoodx.com

The Eastwood Experience is like nothing else. Opened in 2014, the spin studio is tranquil and the amenities are beautiful. There are two options for spin: 'the icon', a music-focused and high-energy class, and 'the athlete', an endurance class. In addition to spin classes they also host guided meditation classes.

448 TIGHT CLUB

5 passionate
LOCAL WINERIES
worth a visit

---

451 BACKYARD VINEYARDS

232 St, #3033
Langley ⑫
+1 604 539 9463
backyardvineyards.ca

Since 2009 Backyard Vineyards has been producing award-winning blended and bubbly wines made from 100% B.C. grapes. The grapes, grown on vineyard, are paired perfectly with fruit from the Fraser Valley and South Okanagan. The tasting room is sophisticated but laidback, cool in the summer and cozy in the winter.

452 CHABERTON ESTATE WINERY

1064 216 St
Langley ⑫
+1 604 530 1736
chabertonwinery.com

Established in 1975 and spreading across 55 acres, this winery is one of the oldest and largest in the province. Home to countless award-winning wines, the hidden gem of this spot is the Bacchus Bistro. Serving 'French with a twist', the bistro overlooks the vineyard and as is expected, the food is paired perfectly with their wine.

453 GLASS HOUSE ESTATE WINERY

23349 0 Avenue
Langley ⑫
+1 604 427 3225
*glasshouseestate
winery.com*

This South Langley boutique winery has a minimalist approach to winemaking using only free-run juices in their process. The family-owned vineyard is stunning, particularly impressive is the large glass greenhouse, which pays homage to the family's history in the greenhouse industry.

454 VANCOUVER URBAN WINERY

55 Dunlevy Avenue
Railtown ⑤
+1 604 566 9463
*vancouverurban
winery.com*

Sharing a space with Belgard Kitchen and Postmark Brewing, Vancouver Urban Winery uses B.C. grapes to produce small-batch, handcrafted wines. Their Railtown tasting room has 36 wines on tap for you to try and the space has an edgy industrial feel.

455 PACIFIC BREEZE WINERY

320 Stewardson
Way, #6
New Westminster ⑫
+1 604 522 2228
pacificbreezewinery.com

Known as the first 'Garagiste' or urban winery in Canada, Pacific Breeze purchase their fruit from select vineyards in B.C., Washington and California. The top-quality fruit is carefully and thoughtfully transformed at their space in New Westminster into the 'full-bodied reds and luscious white wines' they have become internationally known for.

The 5 most
'VERY VANCOUVER'
LOCAL CLUBS

---

456 EAST VANCOUVER RUN CREW

pavementbound.com/crews/east-vancouver-run-crew

These energetic folks hit the pavement every Monday evening and while the runs change weekly, the mantra is always the same: start together, finish together, drink beer together. It's a pressure-free, casual, community-based group that all have a love of running in common. Check their Instagram (*@eastvanrunclub*) to find their next starting location.

457 VAN TAN NUDIST CLUB

Mountain Highway
North Vancouver ⑩
+1 604 980 2400
vantan.ca

Founded in 1939, this is Canada's oldest naturalist club. Spanning roughly three idyllic hectares, the member-owned club is located on the slopes of Mount Frome in North Van and includes a pool, beautiful gardens and lawns, sunbathing decks and visits from woodland creatures. Visitors are welcome, check out their website to find out more.

458 CHASING SUNRISE

chasingsunri.se

Whether you're new to hiking or an expert, there is a hiking club for you in Vancouver. With Chasing Sunrise you'll rise before dawn about once a month, hike up a mountain and watch the sunrise from its highest peak with the best like-minded people. Sign up online to find out about the next hike.

459 VANBREWERS CLUB

vanbrewers.ca

At the bar, brewery or at home, it's no secret Vancouverites are big on their beer! VanBrewers is a group of homebrewing beer enthusiasts. They meet monthly to discuss the craft, latest techniques and taste each others work for feedback. They meet the last Thursday of every month, new members are always welcome.

460 VANCOUVER UKULELE CIRCLE

AT: ST JAMES HALL

3214 W 10th Avenue Kitsilano ⑦

vanukes.ca

The Vancouver Ukulele Circle has been meeting once a month for nearly two decades. The 'just for fun group' meets at St James Hall and plays a selection from their 230-page songbook. All are welcome! Even if you don't play the ukulele you're welcome to come and sing along or just sit and enjoy the happy tunes.

The 5 best
SPAS

---

461 FIG

2050 W 4th Avenue
Kitsilano ⑦
+1 604 423 3881
figface.com

Stepping into Fig feels like stepping into the Emerald City in *The Wizard of Oz*. This beauty stop is beautifully designed and offers top-of-the-line service and treatments, including facials, vitamin and filler injections, and skin analysis sessions.

462 CHI, THE SPA

AT: SHANGRI-LA
1128 W Georgia St
West End ③
+1 604 695 2447
shangri-la.com/
vancouver

Pulling inspiration from the East and West, Chi, The Spa at the Shangri-La Hotel is a sanctuary in the city. Many of the spa treatments are inspired by B.C.'s indigenous traditions and northwest nature. The Sea Therapy Facial uses freshly harvested seaweeds, rich in amino acids and vitamins, firms up your skin and gives you a glow.

463 BIOÉTHIQUE

3578 W 4th Avenue
Kitsilano ⑦
+1 604 558 2008
bioethiquespa.com

This bright and lavish spa is a Kitsilano gem. Bioéthique is completely chemical-free, offering certified organic skin care treatments and using skin rejuvenation technology. Known best for their facials, owner Claudine Michaud has spent over two decades researching and creating organic beauty treatments.

464 JOHN CASABLANCAS SALON & SPA

220 Cambie St, #130
Gastown ①
+1 604 629 1602
jcinstitute.com/
salon-and-spa

A great spot if you're wanting a little pampering but not wanting to pay the price. The John Casablancas Institute in Gastown has been training up some of the city's best stylists, estheticians and masseuses since 1978. The treatments are completed by students and the spa is a little less zen but the price gives you peace of mind.

465 SCANDINAVE SPA WHISTLER

8010 Mons Road
Whistler ⑪
+1 888 935 2423
scandinave.com/
whistler

Located just past Whistler Village, the spa is known for its stunning outdoor Nordic thermal baths used for hydrotherapy. An effective way to release tension and toxins, hydrotherapy is an ancient practice that involves running through a hot-cold-relax cycle. All treatments come with access to the pools, saunas and steam rooms or you can pay just to use them.

461 **FIG**

BLOOD ALLEY

35 RANDOM FACTS AND USEFUL DETAILS

The 5 most **FAMOUS VANCOUVERITES**

466 SETH ROGEN

Prior to making it big, Seth grew up doing stand-up in the clubs around town. Now known for his acting, writing, producing, laugh and love of the weed, he often talks about his love for the city and the jelly donuts from Lee's on Granville Island. For a while his voice could be heard making announcements on the SkyTrain and we have an octopus at the Aquarium named after him.

467 RYAN REYNOLDS

Graduating from Kitsilano Secondary School, Ryan has since become one of Hollywood's leading men. He has written, directed and starred in some major blockbusters, including *Deadpool*, which was filmed entirely in Vancouver. This former Sexiest Man Alive goes by *@vancityreynolds* on Instagram and is a huge Canucks fan.

468 MICHAEL BUBLÉ

Before wanting to become a singer Michael Bublé wanted to become a professional hockey player. The four-time Grammy winner found international fame with the release of his 2005 album *It's Time*. Bublé currently lives in West Vancouver with his wife and kids and while he didn't make it on the ice, he is a part owner of the Vancouver Giants junior hockey team.

469 PAMELA ANDERSON

Known for her modelling, acting and animal activism, Pam's big break came in 1989 at a BC Lions football game. Anderson appeared on the Jumbotron wearing a Labatt beer shirt. She was then hired by Labatt to be a spokesmodel and her career took off from there. Most notably she was a star on the hit series *Baywatch* and a *Playboy* model.

470 BRYAN ADAMS

Starting his music career out of his mother's basement at the age of 14, Adams has sold over 100 million records and is the best-selling Canadian rock artist of all time. Most notably was his 1984 album *Reckless,* which included the songs *Summer of '69, Run to You* and *Heaven.* Adams has been nominated for 15 Grammys and countless other singer-songwriter awards.

The 5 most common
CITY NICKNAMES

---

471 CITY OF GLASS

Both a nickname for the city and a book by famed Vancouver creative, Douglas Coupland. 'City of Glass' refers to the dominant steel and glass architectural aesthetic used primarily in the downtown. To see the 'City of Glass' in its full glory, take a trip into the downtown via the Cambie Street Bridge.

471 CITY OF GLASS

472 RAINCOUVER / RAIN CITY / THE WET COAST

Located in a temperate rainforest, Vancouver on average receives 146 cm of rainfall each year. While Vancouverites might grow tired of the grey and wet of the winter months, we know it's what keeps our city so green and beautiful.

473 VANCITY

Believed to have originated from the Vancouver hip-hop scene, 'Vancity' is used frequently on social media and more informal media to refer to Vancouver. It is also the name of a popular apparel brand, Vancity Original, and can be seen around town on sweatshirts and toques.

474 TERMINAL CITY

Terminal City was the nickname given to Vancouver as the western terminus of the Canadian Pacific Railway (CPR). Primarily used for freight, the CPR was once the only practical way to travel across the country. The railroad was extended to Vancouver following British Columbia joining Confederation in 1871.

475 HOLLYWOOD NORTH

Vancouver is the city that never plays itself. With its varied geography, cheaper Canadian dollar and government subsidies, the city often doubles as other locations and is the third-largest production centre for film and television, behind Los Angeles and New York. Being just a three-hour plane ride and in the same time zone of LA also adds to the allure.

5

ESSENTIAL WEBSITES

476 VANCOUVER TRAILS.COM

You'd be hard-pressed to find a Vancouverite who doesn't use Vancouver Trails or has the app on his/her phone. What started as a photo gallery for local hikes is now a top hiking resource providing trail information, directions, maps, photos and current condition updates and reviews from those who have recently taken to the trail.

477 DAILYHIVE.COM/ VANCOUVER

Operating in Toronto, Calgary, Montreal and Vancouver, the DailyHive creates hyperlocal content on the happenings of each city. Popular on social media and with millennials, DailyHive/Vancouver has a bit of a reputation for overexposing local favourites around town. That being said the media company does deliver some good, up-to-date content.

478 VANCOUVER COFFEESNOB.COM

While remaining anonymous, Vancouver Coffee Snob scours the city on the hunt for the perfect coffee shop. The website is friendly, with an interactive map and lists broken down by neighbourhood and the year's best. The writing is sharp and funny, complemented with beautiful photos, and highlighting not only the coffee but also the food offered by each location.

479 BEERMEBC.COM

With the explosion of the craft beer scene in the last 5 years, it's clear that Vancouver has a passion for beer. *BeerMeBC.com* is B.C.'s most-visited beer evaluation resource. On it, you'll find brewery profiles and reviews, recent news stories, events happening in the beer scene and even job postings.

480 SCOUTMAGAZINE.CA

Launched in 2008, *Scout Magazine* is a great resource for all things food and culture in Vancouver. Curated by writers/photographers Andrew Morrison and Michelle Sproule, the goal of the magazine is to 'scout out' and highlight the best the city has to offer. The Scout team knows the city better than most, has great taste and produces top-quality content.

5 interesting
CITY DETAILS

481 SAM KEE BUILDING
8 W Pender St
Chinatown ②

Purchased in 1903 by the Sam Kee Co., this building holds the Guinness World Record for the 'shallowest commercial building in the world'. Originally a standard size, the lot was cut back with the expansion of the street. The main floor measures 4 feet 11 inches (1,6 metre) in width.

482 BLUE FIRE HYDRANTS
Around Vancouver

Completed in 2003 for 52 million dollars, the city installed a special secondary water piping system. Located far underground, the lines can withstand 8.3-Richter earthquakes and are pressurized at 300 psi (normal is 60-120 psi), allowing the water to reach major heights. An engineering feat, it is also built to handle seawater.

483 DUDE CHILLING PARK
2390 Brunswick St
Mount Pleasant ⑧

Intended as a prank, artist Viktor Briestensky set up a fake sign entitled 'Dude Chilling Park' in reference to the *Reclining Figure* installation by Michael Dennis in the park. A local resident started a petition to have the sign permanently installed and following 1800 signatures, the Park Board agreed.

484 BLOOD ALLEY
Gastown ①

Despite its name, gruesome things didn't take place in this famous Gastown alley. Its actual name is Trounce Alley, however in the 1960-70s during Gastown's restoration the name didn't have the allure they wanted. They began calling it Blood Alley, propagating myths that the name derived from blood flowing from slaughterhouses close by.

485 MOST SUPERCARS PER CAPITA

Keep your eyes peeled, there is some major money driving around the streets of Vancouver. Home to the most supercars per capita, it is reported that there are over 2000 vehicles priced over 150.000 dollar. From Ferraris, to Lamborghinis, McLarens, Rolls-Royces and Bentleys, we've got it all.

481 SAM KEE BUILDING

5 bites of
CANUCKS TRIVIA

486 CLOSE BUT NOT QUITE

Joining the National Hockey League in 1970, the Vancouver Canucks have yet to win the prized Stanley Cup. The team has lost in the finals three times, first against the New York Islanders in 1982, the New York Rangers in 1994 and the Boston Bruins in 2011. However, prior to becoming the Canucks, the Vancouver Millionaires did win it in 1915.

487 MOST FAMOUS PLAYERS

Who the best Canuck of all time is, depends on who you talk to. That being said, standouts include: 'The Russian Rocket' Pavel Bure, top goal scorer Marcus Näslund and 'Captain Canuck' Trevor Linden. We also can't forget Swedish twins Daniel and Henrik Sedin, who played their entire 18-year career in Vancity.

488 THE SEDIN'S LAST GAME STATS

Just a sample of the spooky stats from identical twins Daniel (#22) and Henrik (#33) Sedin's last game: Henrik had 2 assists, Daniel had 2 goals, face-offs were 33-22 Vancouver, #22 scored his first goal 33 seconds into the 3rd period, it was his 22nd goal of the year. His 2nd goal was scored 2:33 into overtime, breaking the 3-3 tie.

489 VIRAL RIOT PHOTO

Snapped by Vancouver photographer Rich Lam during the 2011 Stanley Cup riot, the photo shows a young couple kissing in the street surrounded by cars on fire, riot police and tear gas. The photo received local, national and international attention, gracing the pages of prominent news outlets such as *The Atlantic*, *The Guardian* and the *New York Times*.

490 WHERE TO BUY MERCH

Canucks merchandise can be found in shops all over the city, however for authentic merchandise, head to the Canucks Team Store located in Rogers Arena, where the team plays. There you will find a wide variety of Canucks gear including retro and customized jerseys.

The 5
THINGS TO KNOW
ABOUT BC BUD

491 WHY IT'S CALLED 'BC BUD'?

Officially the name 'BC Bud' refers to any cannabis grown within the province of British Columbia. Generally when the phrase is used however, it also refers to its reputation for being the most potent and best marijuana in the world.

492 420

420 refers to two things. First, it's a name for marijuana that originated from high-school kids in California, who met every day to smoke weed at that time. Now more commonly, it refers to the annual April 20th (4/20) Cannabis Festival. Originally a protest, it is now much more a celebration with over 150.000 people attending the 2019 event on Sunset Beach.

493 LEGALIZATION

The legalization of cannabis in Canada has been a long and arduous process. In 2000, the courts ruled that Canadians had the right to use marijuana as medicine and in 2016 a national poll found 7/10 citizens were in favour of legalization. On October 17, 2018, under Justin Trudeau's Liberal government, the use of recreational cannabis became legal nationwide.

494 WHAT YOU CAN BUY AND WHERE TO BUY IT

While restrictions vary province to province, cannabis leaves, edibles, extracts and topicals can all be legally purchased at government-run stores, licensed private retailers, and the B.C. government's online store. Google the government official interactive map for locations. Additionally, you can also grow four plants per household for recreational use.

495 CBD VS THC

Both cannabidiol (CBD) and tetrahydro-cannabinol (THC) are two natural compounds found in cannabis, THC is the main psychoactive compound and is responsible for the 'high' sensation. CBD has the same chemical formula as THC but with a different atom arrangement and is therefore more commonly used for medical purposes.

5 INSPIRING INITIATIVES

---

496 HIVES FOR HUMANITY

hivesforhumanity.com

Establishing their first honey beehive in 2012 in a public garden on the Downtown Eastside, this non-profit works to foster self-worth and community pride, while also helping the bees. They do this through their community gardening, beekeeping, mentorship programs for at-risk neighbours and community collaborations. The harvested honey is sold locally.

497 A BETTER LIFE FOUNDATION

abetterlife foundation.ca

Operating out of the Save On Meats, A Better Life Foundation works to increase food security for those on hard times. ABLF provides employment opportunities and serves over 850 meals a day through their meal service and token programs. Check out their monthly fundraising event, the Greasy Spoon Diner, where famous chefs cook up a four-course meal to help raise funds.

498 CITY FARMER
cityfarmer.eco

City Farmer is on a mission to show Vancouverites how to grow food, compost waste and take care of their landscape responsibly. The group maintains five gardens around the city: a waterwise native plant garden, a climate change adaptation garden, an organic food garden, an outdoor classroom, and a biodiversity garden. They host tours and classes and operate a gardening hotline.

499 PAWS FOR HOPE ANIMAL FOUNDATION
pawsforhope.org

Paws for Hope is committed to creating and improving sustainable animal welfare in B.C.. The non-profit has a variety of programs aimed to help our furry friends including Roxy's Relief, which provides basic veterinary care to pets of vulnerable individuals who might otherwise not be able to afford it.

500 LOOSE LIPS MAGAZINE
looselipsmag.com

Founded by journalism school grads Brittany Tiplady and Kristi Alexandra, *Loose Lips Magazine* is an online Vancouver-based feminist publication. Employing an intersectional lens, they're on a mission to publish content that represents the womxn of Vancouver. The magazine covers everything from current events and women's health to local art and culture.

STAWAMUS CHIEF

INDEX

COLOPHON

EDITING, COMPOSING *and* PHOTOGRAPHY — Shannon McLachlan

ADDITIONAL PHOTOGRAPHY — p. 216: Kerry Maguire, p. 221: Martin Tessler

GRAPHIC DESIGN — Joke Gossé and Sarah Schrauwen

COVER IMAGE — Lynn Canyon Suspension Bridge (secret 272)

The addresses in this book have been selected after thorough independent research by the author, in collaboration with Luster Publishing. The selection is solely based on personal evaluation of the business by the author. Nothing in this book was published in exchange for payment or benefits of any kind.

D/2020/12.005/2

ISBN 978 94 6058 2639

NUR 513, 510

© 2020 Luster, Antwerp
www.lusterweb.com — WWW.THE500HIDDENSECRETS.COM
info@lusterweb.com

Printed in Italy by Printer Trento.